MOM
TAKE CENTER
STAGE

*Unfiltered. Unapologetic. Unstoppable. A
Guide for Moms Ready to Reclaim the Spotlight.*

Satya V. Nauth

Mom Take Center Stage

Copyright © 2025 by Satya Nauth

ISBN (paperback): 979-8-9994524-1-2

Cover design by Rony Dhar

Printed in the United States of America

This book is dedicated to the woman who has always taken center stage—my mother.

With fire in her eyes and steel in her spine, she showed me what it means to rise, to lead, and to never shrink. She has lived with a warrior's heart, a fearless voice, and a presence that fills the room before she ever speaks. This is her legacy, and I carry it forward.

Table of Contents

Take Center Stage with Me

Before you dive in, I want to invite you to stay connected beyond these pages.

Visit SatyaNauth.com (https://satyanauth.com) to access free resources, behind-the-scenes insights, and weekly encouragement created just for moms like you—those ready to live boldly and lead from within.

Email: MomTakeCenterStage@gmail.com

➜📱 Scan the QR code to connect instantly and to begin your journey now.

Introduction

For many years, I poured out my heart and soul in the name of motherhood. In the process, I lost myself. After having kids, I faced a series of challenges that seemed insurmountable. Those very challenges became the reasons for overcoming obstacles and confidently becoming my authentic self . . . the real *me*. My life used to revolve entirely around my children. They were the center of my universe. I was buried under the chaos that was unravelling right before my eyes. While I loved being a mother, somewhere along the way, I lost sight of who I was.

My days were consumed by endless tasks: work, school drop-offs and pickups, doctor visits, maintaining the household, and juggling countless after-school activities. But I knew motherhood was an investment. It was a bittersweet time though. While I loved raising my kids, I didn't love that I was paying a hefty price through my selflessness. I thought that pursuing my dreams and goals meant giving up on my children, which felt like a betrayal of motherhood. Then it hit me: *One day my children will grow up, and I'll have to face myself again. Who will I be then?* Since children grow up and become adults, I realized I needed to reclaim my individuality. Buried in all those years of dedication, I began to see things more clearly: I needed to muster up the courage to find myself, to become multidimensional, to take center stage.

We are all called to discover our higher purpose. Going through a myriad of emotions, it's easy to play the blame game. Blame the world, blame our health, blame our past, blame current situations, and blame the decisions that have led to this moment. With all that said, I have to ask you: *Mom, isn't it time you took center stage?*

This book is taken from the lessons I have learned through trial and error. It is a daring guide of self-acceptance, personal development, and remarkable success after having children. I'm here as a woman, like you, who has gone through some beautifully chaotic and humbling experiences after having kids. Some difficult growth experiences that have led to establishing my full identity and, at the same time, becoming a better parent. Not as an appendage to my children or spouse but as a confident, bold woman who knows and understands my worth because I have rediscovered *myself.*

Gals, it's pretty easy to close this book and move on to the next thing that calls to us. And with the endless distractions out there, you could head to Facebook, Instagram or TikTok and go down that rabbit hole. Or you could go back to washing that mountain of laundry. This is my call to you: When will you do the things that will allow you to stand on your own feet? When will you be daringly bold? When is the right time for you? I'll tell you: *That time is now.* It's today. It is in this moment. This is your chance to finally become who you were meant to be.

Life is unpredictable, so what I'm asking of you isn't a cutesy idea. It is a life skill that we as women and as mothers need to impart not only to ourselves, but also to our children. Be prepared before the necessity becomes desperation. Be an example to your kids. Show them that this valiant woman is also in charge of her life, her autonomy, her decisions. She isn't afraid to dream, set goals, and go forth.

This guide is intended not only for the two of us. It is also meant for every woman who needs to hear that she is enough, that there is hope to learn, to grow, and to achieve everything her heart calls to irrespective of age, status, skin color, religion, or any difference that makes you one in a million. Anything that makes you stand out is your superpower! Let's embark on this journey together. I can't wait to see the woman you'll rediscover—the bold, confident, and unstoppable YOU.

What Moms Are Saying

Below are anonymous posts from moms of various mom groups. I have altered any information that appeared to be sensitive information.

HE THREATENED DIVORCE. THAT I'LL BE FORCED TO GET A JOB. I HAVE WORKED SINCE HIGH SCHOOL. I HAVE ALWAYS HAD MY OWN MONEY AND WORKED UNTIL GIVING BIRTH. MY HEART IS HURTING.

UGH, I'M SO DEFLATED. I'M THE HEAVIEST I'VE EVER BEEN. MY CONFIDENCE IS GONE. MY CLOTHES DON'T FIT, AND I NEED TO LOSE WEIGHT.

I CAN'T DO IT ANYMORE. I HAVE THREE KIDS. SOMEBODY IS ALWAYS SCREAMING OR CRYING. SOMETIMES IT'S ME. I'M EXHAUSTED. I WORK FULL TIME. I FEEL LIKE I HAVE NO SUPPORT. I'M ANXIOUS, STRESSED, FRUSTRATED, TIRED, ANGRY, AND SAD.

I HAVE NO IDEA WHAT TO DO. I'M REALLY STRUGGLING. I'M A SINGLE MOM OF THREE, I'M SO TIRED. I LEFT A DOMESTIC ABUSIVE RELATIONSHIP, AND I REGRET IT EVERYDAY. I'M FAR BEHIND ON BILLS AND RENT. I'M DROWNING. I HAVE NO SUPPORT.

I'M A STAY AT HOME MOM. WE HAVE BILLS, RENT, CAR PAYMENT, SCHOOL LOANS...I FEEL SO STRESSED OUT. I NEED TO MAKE MORE MONEY! I DON'T KNOW WHAT TO DO. I FEEL SO OVERWHELMED!

Part One

The Dress Rehearsal:
Behind the Curtain

Chapter One

Winning over the Greatest Critic

Loving yourself isn't vanity. It's sanity.

—Katrina Mayer

I caught a glimpse of myself in the mirror the other day—hair unkempt, eyes tired, and a familiar voice in my head whispering, *Not enough.* It wasn't my spouse, my friends, my in-laws, or anyone else criticizing me. It was me. And isn't that always the case? Your greatest critic isn't someone else. It's you. No one can tear you down like you can. Why is that? Because no one knows you better than you. So when you err—as you will because you are human—you tend to communicate your displeasure and replay those thoughts on repeat in your mind.

Have you ever had a song stuck in your head, playing over and over until it drives you crazy? Right now, there's a tune from my workout playlist that I can't seem to shake. It's frustrating, isn't it? Now imagine if, instead of a song, it was a loop of negative, self-defeating thoughts hammering away in your mind. If someone else spoke to you that way, you'd be outraged. Yet we tolerate this from ourselves every day.

Motherhood can challenge *any* woman because it changes everything: our bodies, our emotions, our mindset, even our aspirations. Childbirth leaves its mark, and for many of us, the physical changes can feel like a heavy toll. The hips widen, the hormones spiral, metabolism morphs into a monstrous sloth-like creature. Don't even get me started on the good and bad "wolf" inside us that changes our emotions on a dime. And let's be real: The pooch is here. In essence, it's a badge of honor, a reminder that we carried life within us for nine straight months, giving our all to nourish the human we conceived. For those who've mastered the pooch acceptance, kudos to you. But for the rest of us? Let's start embracing it for what it is: a symbol of strength and sacrifice. The journey back to yourself starts with one thing: love. Not love for your spouse, your kids, or your friends, though all of those things matter. I'm talking about self-love, the kind we rarely prioritize.

Self-love is not an easy endeavor. We're our own harshest critic, constantly finding fault in our appearance, our decisions, and the way we handle life. Compliments from others? They're no match for the voice we hear when we look in the mirror. That internal scolding is the omnipotent power that rules our minds, hearts, and lives. Starting today, though, I challenge you to change the message your inner dialogue is sending.

Your Body, Your Naos: A Sacred Space

I used to think of self-care as a luxury—something that came after I had taken care of everything and everyone else. But over time, I realized that neglecting myself was not noble; it was destructive. My body, my mind, and my spirit suffered as a result. Then I came across a word that shifted my entire perspective: *naos*.

In ancient Greek, *naos* means "temple," but not just any temple. It refers to the inner sanctuary, the most sacred place in a place of worship. The part that is revered, protected, and honored above all else. That struck me. Because if we only have one body, one vessel to carry us through this life, shouldn't we treat it with the same level of respect as a sacred temple?

I'm sure you pour your energy endlessly into others, but what if you saw yourself as a naos—something precious, something worth tending to with care and intention? Just as you work to be mentally strong, you also owe it to yourself to be physically and emotionally strong. That might mean you need to transform your perspective on strength. Instead of martyrdom and sacrifice being what you attribute to inner strength, see strength as vitality, endurance, and the ability to show up fully for the life you are building.

Eye Contact: The Power of Connection

When was the last time you looked yourself in the eye—without makeup, without filters, without judgement. What did you see? The eyes are often said to be windows to the soul, but for many of us, it's hard to look so directly at ourselves, especially after the changes motherhood brings. Avoiding eye contact, whether with others or when facing your reflection in the mirror, can be a sign that self-love is a challenge. But recognizing your avoidance is the first step toward overcoming it.

Here's a daily practice to help you remember your strength, your worth, and who you really are: Stand in front of a mirror, look into your eyes, and say something kind to yourself. Yes, it might feel awkward at first. But over time, you'll start to believe it. The simple act of meeting your gaze with kindness can shift your mindset in profound ways. The truth is, you matter. You are beautiful and *enough* just as you are right now, in this moment. So take a chance on yourself. Give yourself the love you hope to receive from others and yourself.

Beyond the Surface

As moms, we pour so much of ourselves into others that our own cups often runneth dry. Physical and mental self-care should go beyond occasional indulgences. They should be a foundation for strength, resilience, and well-being. We have one body, one mind. Just like a car that needs regular maintenance to perform at its best, we need intentional care to thrive.

Physical Self-Care: Vitality over Vanity

Physical self-care isn't about trying to have an ageless face, a perfect body, or the most expensive spa treatment. It's about vitality. It's about honoring the vessel (our naos) that carries you through life. We often focus on the outward appearance, but true physical self-care begins from within. Start by nourishing your body with wholesome food, moving it with intention, and prioritizing rest. Your body is designed to carry you through long days, but it needs fuel, movement, and restoration to continue performing at its best.

How often do you listen to your body when it's telling you it's tired, or when it craves fresh air or a healthy meal? Sometimes self-care looks like saying no to the things that drain you and yes to the things that recharge your energy—whether it's a ten-minute walk outside, taking a restorative nap, or making time for a workout that challenges you.

Consider how movement can become an act of self-love. Don't see it as simply burning calories or trying to fit into a certain size. Aim to feel strong, capable, and energized. Whether it's yoga, dancing to your favorite song, or lifting weights, find a way to move that makes your body feel powerful and alive.

Style Rituals: Confidence in the Details

Embodying a unique sense of style after having kids takes a lot more time and effort. It's easy to skip, but the way you care for yourself directly impacts how you feel about yourself. That feeling of washing your face, styling your hair, or putting on an outfit that makes you feel good is a signal to yourself that you matter.

For me, it's high heels. Just shy of five foot three, wearing heels makes me feel confident and bold. I can walk into any room, head held high, and hold my own. I'm not trying to impress anyone else; I simply love how the heels make me feel. What gives you that sassy flare, that extra enthusiasm, that tilt in your hips when you walk? For me, a fiery-red lipstick is a tool of empowerment. On tough days, I challenge myself to get up, get dressed, and put on my best shoes. The higher the heel, the better. And you know what? It works.

Find the style ritual that makes you feel like the best version of yourself. Whether it's a bold lipstick, a favorite outfit, or a particular accessory, it's about connecting with the woman inside who is strong, confident, and ready to conquer whatever comes her way.

REFLECTIONS

1. *Be Aware of Eye Contact:* Start each day by standing in front of a mirror and making eye contact with yourself. Say something kind, affirming your worth and power. This simple act of self-connection can shift your mindset and strengthen your inner dialogue.

Action Step: Each morning, take thirty seconds to lock eyes with your reflection and speak words of kindness to yourself. Feel the power of your own gaze.

2. *Prioritize Physical and Mental Self-Care:* Your body and mind are the foundation of everything you do. Remember, you only have one body, so treat it like a naos (your sacred sanctuary). Prioritize rituals that support both physical and mental health. In doing so, you are nurturing your vitality and well-being.

Action Step: Dedicate time to intentional physical care, whether it's a short walk, stretching, or setting intentions for your day. Combine this with a mental health practice, such as journaling or visualization, to feel grounded and ready.

3. *Establish Style Rituals*: The way you care for yourself impacts how you feel. Style rituals—whether it's your signature lipstick, the outfit that makes you feel powerful, or the shoes that give you confidence—are a form of self-respect. These rituals are more than appearance; they signal to yourself that you are worthy and capable.

Action Step: Find one ritual that makes you feel empowered and commit to it each day. Whether it's styling your hair, applying your favorite lipstick, or wearing your go-to heels, let this ritual be your reminder of your strength and confidence.

4. *Embrace the Journey to Self-Love:* Winning over your harshest critic (yourself) requires daily practices that prioritize self-love and connection. Change happens when we commit to habits that nurture our well-being, mind, and spirit.

Action Step: Choose one new habit from this chapter to implement each day. Be consistent, and remind yourself that you are enough—just as you are. The journey back to yourself starts today.

TAKEAWAYS

- *You are not your harshest thoughts.* You are the voice that can replace them.

- *Your body is not a burden.* It is a sacred space, your naos, worthy of care and reverence.

- *The mirror doesn't reflect flaws*; it reflects a woman who keeps showing up. That's power!

- *Caring for yourself physically boosts vitality.* Strength is your birthright, not a bonus.

- *Style rituals aren't superficial.* They're daily reminders that you matter, that you deserve to feel good.

- *Self-love is not a luxury.* It is a necessity, a discipline, and a daily practice.

- *The journey to loving yourself starts with awareness*, but it blooms through action.

Chapter Two

Supermom Habits

Being a parent is dirty and scary and beautiful and hard and miraculous and exhausting and thankless and joyful and frustrating all at once. It's everything.
—Jill Smokler

I often reminisce about life before kids and how those cute, rambunctious little monsters hijack most of my time. Pre-motherhood, losing a few pounds or getting in shape wasn't even a thought. It was "totes easy," as the kids say today. Fast-forward to motherhood, and we moms are busier than ever. Creating healthy habits and sticking to them isn't as simple anymore.

Somewhere along the way, we became second to our little ones. They are our first priority, yet we sometimes forget that we matter too. New moms often feel like their hands are more than full. Moms of toddlers run around like chickens with their heads cut off. And if your kids are preteens or teens, it doesn't get any easier.

At every stage, we are juggling everyone else's needs while trying to figure out how to balance life, stay sane, be healthy, and—this is a big one—love ourselves unconditionally. Truth be told, we're busy! Aren't we, gals? We may not notice when the sun sets, but we sure know when it rises! Just as time never stops, we keep tick-tocking! You are a supermom because no one handles life quite like you.

The Pooch and the Pressure

Is your metabolism not what it used to be? Our bodies don't bounce back the way they did in our teens and twenties. Let's talk about the pooch. You know the one. That stubborn belly fat that refuses to budge no matter what we do. I know there are some fabulous, fit moms out there killing it on Instagram. They seem to have mastered the pooch problem. And hey, we're a bit jealous, aren't we? How did they do it? Why is theirs gone and mine is lingering? But here's the thing: Your health, your body, and your confidence should be defined by you—not by society's impossible beauty standards.

The goal here is self-acceptance for where you are today. It's important to be present in your body without falling into the trap of comparison, shame, and harsh judgement. Doing so requires a shift in what you've been told is beautiful and acceptable. Redefine beauty in the truest sense, and you'll discover that it radiates from within and places self-love above all else. In time, you will intuit what diet, exercise routine, and weight suits you best because it will come easily and without stress. Follow the prompt of your inner self, not society, and it will lead you to a body that is uniquely yours and feels right. It won't likely be the twenty-year-old version, but that's the point. You are always changing, so it makes sense that your body will undergo some transformations too. Learning to embrace this evolution rather than resist it, frees you up to focus on what really matters. . Because you matter. Your health matters. And I want you to live your best life—one filled with vibrant experiences, travel, and joy.

The Power of Self-Talk

You might be surprised to know this, but we talk to ourselves more than anyone else. Whether we're celebrating a win or analyzing a loss, we're constantly narrating our lives. We praise or appraise our own performance. If we're not careful, our minds can beat us down mentally, taking defeats or losses quite personally. Those peculiar, pestering thoughts seep into the recesses of our mind and bombard us. And if we're not careful, those inner conversations can turn toxic.

Take the loss of a relationship or a friendship that no longer served you. Even if you know it was the right decision, negative thoughts can creep in, making you second-guess yourself. Thoughts may be intangible, but if you act on them, they mold your reality. You have a choice: Speak to yourself with kindness and encouragement, or mentally tear yourself down.

The "I Am" Habit

Developing an "I am" habit can transform how you see and treat yourself. Speak to yourself in the positive present tense:

- *I am* confident.

- *I am* making healthy decisions.

- *I am* a great writer.

This simple habit eliminates the negative self-talk that says, "I am not good enough," or "I am not going to succeed." Think of your mind like a garden. You wouldn't plant weeds in your garden, so why allow negative thoughts to take root in your mind?

Research supports this approach. A study from the University of Cambridge found that suppressing negative thoughts can improve mental health, even for those struggling with PTSD. Contrary to popular belief, suppressing unwanted thoughts reduces their power over time, leading to improved emotional well-being. Professor Michael Anderson, who led the study, explained: "We've been told that suppressing thoughts is ineffective and makes people think about them more—like the classic, 'Don't think about a pink elephant.' However, our research shows that suppressing negative thoughts actually improved mental health outcomes."[1]

Be Your Own Mental Mentor

We often look to others for motivation, but what if you became your own source of encouragement? One powerful technique is addressing yourself in the third person during stressful moments. Instead of saying, "I can't do this," say, "You've got this. Breathe deeply and stay calm." It may feel odd at first, but research suggests that speaking to yourself in the third person creates emotional distance, helping you process feelings more objectively.

Trust Your Inner Compass

You have an internal compass—a guiding intuition that's always trying to lead you in the right direction. Think about Captain Jack Sparrow in *Pirates of the Caribbean*. He never let go of his magical compass because he believed it would always lead him to what he truly wanted. You have that same inner compass. But unlike Jack's, yours won't be stolen. When you listen to your instincts and trust yourself, life's path becomes clearer.

Building Transformational Habits

As moms, our schedules revolve around our kids. Finding time for wellness and self-care often feels impossible.

But I've learned that small, daily habits can create extraordinary results. For example, I've been taking daily walks for over ten years. It started with a simple decision to make time for myself. I replaced my afternoon nap with a thirty-minute walk, and now it's a nonnegotiable habit.

Habit to Change	Replacement Habit
Oversleeping	Getting to sleep earlier
Procrastination	Following a set schedule
Excessive napping	Going for a walk

REFLECTIONS

Your "I Am" List

By changing negative self-talk and building positive routines, you can create a healthier, more fulfilling life.

On a blank sheet of paper, create three columns:

I Am	I Am Not	I Am Working On
I am an author.	I am not shy.	I am writing daily for thirty minutes.

Fill in three to five items under each column. Then do the following:

- Embody your "I am."

- Eliminate your "I am not."

- Make progress on your "I am working on."

With intentional effort, you'll transform your mindset and your life.

TAKEAWAYS

- *Habits don't have to be perfect*—they just have to start. Small shifts lead to big changes.

- *Your self-talk is shaping your story.* Speak to yourself with the same love you give others.

- *The "I am" habit is a mindset game-changer.* What you affirm, you become.

- *Body comparison steals your joy.* Health is about vitality, not vanity.

- *Replace guilt with grace.* You're doing your best, and that's enough.

- *Your intuition is a compass.* Trust it. Follow it. It's never steered you wrong.

- *You already have the power.* You just need a plan—and belief—to unlock it.

Chapter Three

Getting Rid of Irrational Fears

Hope begins in the dark.
—Anne Lamott

The quote above from Anne Lamott captures the journey so many of us face as mothers, especially when fear feels louder than hope. Fear sneaks into our lives the moment we become moms. It's a natural response that helps us recognize potential threats and protect ourselves and our children. When we become mothers, our instinct to shield our little ones goes into overdrive. I know this because I am a mom to two boys I fiercely protect!

Sometimes, though, fear storms in. It takes over when you're facing something that feels too big to fix: a medical diagnosis, intense bullying, your teen experimenting with drugs or slipping away into rebellion. You're doing your best, setting boundaries, showing up, praying, pleading—and yet you still feel powerless. That hopelessness creeps in with the late-night questions we never say out loud: *What if they never come back? What if they hate me for intervening? What if I lose them?*

Fear becomes a problem when it shifts from being a helpful safeguard to an irrational force that dictates our every move. We've brought human beings into this world, and yes, we would move mountains for their safety!

But here's the catch: What we fear, we pass on. When we let imagined fears take the wheel, those anxieties imprint on our children. If we constantly say no, reprimand too often, or overreact to everyday mishaps, we may unintentionally be teaching them to live in fear rather than confidence.

That's not to say we shouldn't correct bad behavior. If your toddler smears soggy Cheetos on the wall, how do you react? Do you scold out of instinct, or do you handle it calmly? How about if your child falls? Do you automatically go into fight-or-flight mode, or do you pause before reacting?

As parents, our automatic programming often leans toward scolding and saying no. Children's brains aren't fully developed. They don't always understand right from wrong. While it's important to establish rules and discipline, the word *no* should not become the default language of our parenting.

Try reframing your response. When my son fell as a toddler, I'd say "Wow, that was a cool move!" or "Great job getting back up!" If he was genuinely hurt, I'd kiss his boo-boos and comfort him, but I avoided turning every stumble into a catastrophe. This calm approach helps kids develop resilience, and it might help steady your nerves too. Taking center stage in your life means showing up with intention—even in the everyday chaos of spills, tantrums, and scraped knees.

Momxiety: When Worry Takes Over

Momxiety is that nagging mix of worry, nervousness, and unease that shows up the moment you become a mother. It's that constant inner chatter: *Is the baby breathing? Did I sanitize the bottle enough? Am I doing this right?* It starts early and can easily spiral into an all-consuming cycle of fear.

Now, don't get me wrong: It's normal to be protective, especially in today's world. The COVID-19 pandemic heightened our awareness of germs, and some caution is healthy. But here's the hard truth: Worrying doesn't solve problems; it creates them. It raises your stress levels, steals joy from moments you should be savoring, and worst of all, it can create a domino effect of anxiety that spills over into your children's lives.

Safety Momxiety

Do you have overblown fears of some catastrophe happening to your child or family? You might obsess that the garage door was left open, the alarm wasn't set, or the house isn't secure enough. I can attest to leaving my bedroom door open so I can hear my boys if they need me—or closing all the blinds in case someone might be watching me from the outside. These fears feel real in the moment, but often they're just imagined projections of what-if scenarios.

Living this way wears us out and teaches our kids to live on the edge of constant fear. If your anxiety feels overwhelming, consider seeking professional support.

Getting your fears in check helps not only you but also your family.

Association Momxiety

This anxiety revolves around the people we allow near our children. Do they need to be constantly vetted and monitored? Sometimes, yes. If your gut tells you something is off, trust it. I remember years ago, a gentleman gave me the creeps whenever he was around my kids. I quickly stopped all association because my intuition was clear: Something was wrong! Never second-guess your instincts. That said, we shouldn't automatically view everyone with suspicion. Having a constant fear or distrust of people teaches our children that the world is unsafe. Trust your instincts, but balance them with rational thinking. Teach your kids to be cautious, not fearful.

Momxiety→ Childhood Anxiety→ Adult Anxiety

Anxiety doesn't just appear one day. It is built over a lifetime of experiences. A child raised in an environment of constant fear or negativity internalizes those patterns and carries them into adulthood.

Imagine this: A parent projects unease onto their child, unintentionally imprinting fear-based behaviors. That child grows into a teen who is anxious and uncertain, and by adulthood, they have deeply ingrained fears that they don't even realize were modeled to them.

Children are expert observers. Paired with what we say, they listen and pay attention to how we react to everyday life encounters. They are influenced by how we handle stress, how we interact with others, and how we view life as something to either fear or embrace. They do as we do, not necessarily as we say. As moms, we must be diligent in recognizing these generational patterns. By managing our fears and anxieties, we give our children the tools to grow into confident, resilient adults. Therefore it's important to be mindful of our nuanced behaviors that send the wrong message.

Children are sponges for not only knowledge but emotions, energy, and behaviors. You are your child's first mirror. They don't just hear what you say; they see *how* you say it. If you approach a problem rationally and with confidence, they'll also internalize those traits. But if you consistently respond with panic, anger, or fear, they are likely to reflect that behavior too. Whether it's worrying over scraped knees or panicking over whether your teen will come home safe, our anxiety writes the early scripts our children will carry with them.

The Power of Your Reactions

Imagine your child scrapes their knee. If you rush over in a panic, they'll likely burst into tears—even if it wasn't that bad. But if you stay steady and say, "Oops, that was a good fall! Let's check it out," they are more likely to brush it off and move on.

I remember the scene like it was yesterday. My boys were playing on the bed, and my little one's teeth bit all the way through his tongue. I was alarmed that he was hurt, but I didn't overreact. When he saw that I didn't panic, he responded in kind. I took him to the emergency room, and he remained calm the entire time. I was so impressed! Though I can imagine a different outcome if I had overreacted and panicked.

Your reactions teach resilience. They show your child how to handle challenges, big and small. The tone of your voice carries weight—sometimes more than the words themselves. A sharp tone can feel like a reprimand, even if you're simply saying, "Pick that up!" A gentle tone, on the other hand, makes requests feel like invitations instead of demands.

Your Cues Shape Their Future

Your child is learning to interpret the world through your actions and energy. Every expression, reaction, and vocal tone teaches them something—whether it's resilience, confidence, or anxiety. By being mindful of your visual and mental cues, you are raising a self-aware and emotionally secure child, and also building a healthier dynamic for yourself.

This isn't about perfection. It's about awareness. Every small shift in your responses—pausing before reacting, softening your tone, approaching challenges with calmness—creates a ripple effect that shapes your child's emotional intelligence and overall well-being. If you're having difficulty reining in your reactive emotions, I encourage you to develop a self-check system to help you retrain your autopilot responses. In doing so, you are also retraining your kids as well.

First, identify your triggers. Write down three situations where you often feel reactive. Then, design alternative ways to respond that are reasonable for each situation that shift you into intentional parenting instead of reacting out of fear or anger. Here is a framework to follow:

● *Pause before reacting*: Take a deep breath before responding to a frustrating situation. A two-second pause can mean the difference between an impulsive reaction and a thoughtful response.

● *Reframe the message*: Swap criticism for encouragement. Instead of saying, "You are so messy!" say, "Oops, let's clean this up together."

● *Model problem-solving*: When things go wrong, verbalize your thought process. "Hmm, this spilled juice is a mess. Let's grab some paper towels and fix it." This teaches kids problem-solving and resourcefulness.

● *Check your energy*: Your mood sets the tone. At the end of the day, reflect on how your emotions shaped your child's behavior. If you were stressed, think of small shifts to reset for tomorrow.

Before I began this journey, I reacted from a place of overwhelm. But stepping into my power meant learning to pause, to breathe, and to choose my response. That power pause has provided strength. It's the sacred space where growth lives—for both me and my children.

REFLECTIONS

Rewiring Your Reactions

Use this worksheet to become more aware of your responses and create new, constructive habits.

Trigger	Usual Response	Child's Reaction	Alternative Response	Expected Outcome
You see spilled juice on the floor.	"Be careful! You're so messy!"	Child cries, feels ashamed.	"Let's clean it up together."	Child learns mistakes are okay and fixable.
Your child is dangerously climbing a chair.	"Get down right now! You're going to fall and get hurt!"	Child feels fearful and hesitant.	"That looks tricky! Let's find a safer way to climb."	Child develops confidence and problem-solving skills instead of reacting in fear.

1. Replace my examples with real-life scenarios that trigger your reactive response.

2. Be honest about how your child typically reacts to your fear triggers.

3. Brainstorm and practice new responses to create a more positive pattern.

4. Reflect on any changes in your child's behavior after implementing these shifts.

TAKEAWAYS

- *Your reactions shape their world*: Children mirror your behavior. Respond with calmness and intention.

- *Recognize healthy fear versus irrational fear*: Sometimes fear is necessary, but often it creates unnecessary anxiety.

- *Mistakes are learning moments*: Show your child how to handle challenges instead of fearing them.

- *You are your child's first role model*: Your body language, words, and tone teach them how to navigate life.

- *Change starts small*: One mindful response at a time can reshape your child's emotional development.

How you respond in everyday chaotic moments reshapes your kids *and* you. Every calm response, every reframed reaction is a step toward the woman you are becoming. You are rising into a more powerful self as you raise your kids. And that is part of you taking center stage.

Chapter Four

It's Okay Not to Be Okay

Sometimes the fall kills you. And sometimes, when you fall, you fly.
—*Neil Gaiman*

Taking center stage doesn't mean you'll always have it together. Sometimes, it means standing in your truth even when things feel messy, tired, or unsure. If I had a dollar for every time I needed to hear, "It's okay not to be okay" as a mom, I'd probably be swimming in riches. In today's world, where perfection is curated, filtered, and hashtagged, it's hard not to feel like we're failing at every turn. We need to differentiate between *actual* perfection and *perceived* perfection.

Social media might be a playground for inspiration, but it's also a breeding ground for comparison. And I speak truth when I say *comparison is a thief of joy*. What we see on our screens is the highlight reel, a carefully crafted version of someone's life that conveniently leaves out the meltdowns, fears, anxieties, and sleepless nights.

Rarely do we see the unedited truth. And even when vulnerability does show up, it's often a polished retelling where the context is removed and the rawness softened. We simply can't compete with perfected, filtered, and AI-enhanced lives. And the danger? It damages our self-worth, leaving us questioning if we're doing enough or *being* enough. Judgement comes cheap in this world. But compassionate understanding is rare, and it's golden.

Compassion over Judgement

One time I was at the park with my kids and saw a mom desperately trying to calm her toddler during a meltdown. Her face was flushed with embarrassment, and her eyes darted anxiously at the judging stares around her. Some were disapproving; others awkwardly avoided eye contact. I felt for her because I had been her just a few months ago. One of my sons had thrown a tantrum so epic that I ended up crying in my car afterward. When I saw this woman struggling, I walked over to her, smiled, and said, "You're doing great. We've all been there." The relief on her face was instant.

Once you have been in the trenches, you can see how far any kindness we offer another can go. While compassion takes effort, judgement does not. It's easy to look at someone else's chaos—whether it's their messy house, weight gain, or struggles with anxiety—and roll our eyes. But true strength lies in understanding someone's perspective rather than condemning them.

There's an old saying in Guyana, where I come from: "We cry for our own calf." It means that we naturally show love and leniency to our own, yet when it comes to others, we're quick to criticize. What if we extended the same grace to others that we offer our own child? What if we chose kindness over critique? Trust me, genuine compassion can't be faked. It's a superpower, and the world needs more of it.

New Mom Realities

Becoming a mom is life-changing, and no one prepares you for just how *messy* that change can be. Your body stretches in ways you didn't know were possible, you start sporting raccoon eyes overnight, your metabolism slows to a crawl, and your nights become an endless cycle of diapers, drool, and tears (sometimes the baby's, and sometimes yours). One time I spent twenty minutes trying to console my baby in the middle of the night. The lights were dimmed, and I was in mechanical mode. Little did I realize I'd been feeding him an empty bottle the entire time. Yep, I'd reached peak exhaustion. No one sees the unglamorous side of motherhood—the exploding diapers, the baby puke on your favorite shirt, or the sleep deprivation that makes you question every decision you've ever made. And yet, despite all of this, you're doing an *amazing* job.

So let me say this loud and clear: *It's okay not to be okay.* You're not failing; you're just human. Even when you feel like you're merely surviving, you're still taking center stage because showing up for your child and yourself is a powerful act of courage.

Opinions Are like Armpits

Everyone's got opinions, and sometimes they stink. New moms can expect an avalanche of unsolicited advice. The neighbor swears by her folklore sleep schedule, the family elder is still quoting parenting tips from the 1970s, and the childless friend has an expert take on breastfeeding. Suddenly, everyone's an expert on *your baby*.

I want to remind you of your personal power, especially once you enter parenthood. You don't need to be swayed by anyone's opinion unless you are seeking advice. Being a new mom means trusting your intuition to do what you feel is right for your child and yourself. Don't be swayed by those who guilt you into following a certain parenting method, feeding schedule, educational path, or even a friend group that doesn't vibe with your personality and beliefs.

Most of the opinions we receive come from people who probably shouldn't be giving advice in the first place. And let's be real, it's usually the people closest to us. You can't stop their opinions from flying at you, but you can decide which ones deserve your attention. Some don't even deserve a response. If someone has the audacity to tear you down, they don't have the capacity to see the positive. Smile, nod, and move forward with unshakable mom confidence. You've got this.

Your body has just done the impossible; it stretched, shifted, and made space for life. Some of us shed our baby weight quickly; some don't. Some of us bounce back quickly, and some of us take our sweet time. Maybe your pooch stays, and maybe it goes. Do your best to heal and take care of yourself, but never entertain the idea that weight gain or body changes represent a personal failure. You literally built a human. *Your worth isn't up for debate.*

The Trap of *Buts*

Beware of the sneaky *but*. You know the one. Someone gives you a compliment, and just when you're about to bask in it, they tack on a "but." "You look great for having a baby, *but* have you thought about dieting?" Or "You're doing such a good job as a mom, *but* don't forget about your husband."

That little word carries enough weight to crush your confidence if you let it. A backhanded compliment is not a compliment; it's a critique dressed up in fake encouragement. Recognize these comments for what they are: unnecessary noise. You don't have to absorb every opinion thrown your way. Not every piece of feedback deserves a seat at your table. Build your emotional firewall, and surround yourself with voices that uplift. Let the rest fade into irrelevance.

Stop Comparing and Start Celebrating

Comparison is a trap, and if you are not careful, it will snare you before you even realize what's happening. Maybe it's seeing another mom "bounce back" in record time while you're still figuring out how to feel like yourself again. Maybe it's scrolling through picture-perfect social media posts, wondering why your reality feels so different.

Healing after childbirth is not a competition. Some moms shed baby weight fast. Some don't. Some feel like themselves again in weeks; others take years. Your journey is uniquely yours. Embrace it, imperfections and all. Instead of comparing, start celebrating. Your body grew a human. Your mind and heart are adjusting to an entirely new reality. That's powerful. That's enough.

You can't control other people's opinions, nor can you stop them from comparing you to others. But you can choose which voices you listen to. You don't owe anyone an explanation for how you parent or how you navigate this chapter of your life. The opinions that matter most come from those who truly support you. Let the rest fade into the background where they belong.

REFLECTIONS

Build Your Emotional Confidence Firewall

Take a moment to reflect on how you respond to opinions, comparisons, and judgements.

1. *Make a List of Your Wins*

Write down five things you've done *right* as a mom, no matter how small. Maybe it's how you navigated a sleepless night or the way you got your cranky child to laugh. Celebrate these victories.

2. *Identify Your Trusted Voices*

Think about the people whose opinions truly matter—those who uplift and encourage you. Write down their names. These are the voices to turn to when you need advice or validation.

3. *Create a Mental Shield*

The next time someone offers an unsolicited opinion or makes a backhanded comment, visualize a shield around yourself. Imagine their words bouncing off harmlessly. Then, silently remind yourself: *I am enough.*

4. *Practice Gratitude*

Each night, jot down one thing you're grateful for about yourself. Maybe it's your patience, your strength, or even your ability to laugh through chaos. By embracing these practices, you'll build a strong foundation of self-love and perseverance, no matter what life (or social media) throws your way. You don't owe the world perfection. *You owe yourself grace.*

Reframe Your Shame

1. *Reflect*: Identify a situation where you felt judged, compared yourself to others, or were overly critical of yourself.

2. *Reframe and take action*: Shift your perspective by finding a more compassionate response to help you move forward.

Situation	Reframe and Take Action
You take a break for self-care, and someone implies you should be spending time with your child instead.	"Taking care of myself makes me a better mom. Rest is not a luxury but a necessity."

Situation	Reframe and Take Action
You return to work and feel guilty about leaving your baby.	"I am providing for my family and setting an example of strength. My love is not measured by hours spent together."
Recall of a time you felt judged or doubted yourself.	(Your Reframe and Action Step) How can you shift your mindset and move forward?
Recall a moment when you felt inadequate as a mom.	(Your Reframe and Action Step) Replace self-doubt with self-affirming truth.

TAKEAWAYS

- *Embrace imperfection*: Know that life (and motherhood) is messy. Perfection is a myth. Steady progress is the real win.

- *Focus on your wins*: Every day, write down at least one thing you did well, no matter how small.

- *Guard your energy*: Not all opinions deserve your attention. Decide which voices matter, and let go of the rest.

- *Celebrate others without comparing*: Recognize that someone else's success doesn't diminish your own.

- *Build your emotional firewall*: When faced with negativity, visualize a shield protecting your confidence and self-worth.

- *Recognize that you are doing sacred work*, even when you're doubting yourself. You are growing, becoming, and showing up. And that's what it means to take center stage.

Chapter Five

Cut Yourself Some Serious Slack

Women are smarter by basic instinct and by what we have to do to multitask at home and at work. My mother did that fifty years ago, but it wasn't called multitasking or stress back then. She had a job, two kids and the meals to make with no cook or maid. My father would come home every day and expect lunch. He was a nice guy, but he was clueless!

—Mireille Guiana

If you're like me, cutting yourself slack doesn't come naturally. Since becoming a mom, I've been my toughest critic. Does this sound familiar? As moms, we juggle everything—stimulating our kids with endless activities, handling tantrums with saint-like patience, maintaining a career, keeping our messy homes livable, and trying to carve out time to take care of ourselves (if we're lucky). We run ourselves ragged, trying to keep up with keeping up, only to feel like we're constantly falling short. We become octopus moms, juggling task after task, and even those eight tentacles don't feel like enough. Yes, things need to get done, but have we ever stopped to ask, "What actually needs to get done?"

Do I Really Need To Do That?

External pressure (from "well meaning" family and friends) and self-imposed pressure (yep, that's you) will have you believing you must perform at optimal levels every day. And what happens when you fail to meet these unattainable goals? You become grumpy, irritable, and heap on the shame. I'm here to say that no one can take center stage in that mindset. Instead, set the bar at a realistic level and readjust your priorities, knowing that some days will flow easier and you'll have more energy, while others will get off track due to the unpredictable nature of motherhood and everything else that is on your plate. Be open to "good enough for now," and you'll encounter more wins and stave off any shame that tries to set in. Remember, this is about choosing presence over perfection in a season that demands flexibility.

When you reframe your daily priorities, ask yourself, *How important is it that I do* _____ *right now?*

Do I really need to:

- Wash another load of laundry this second?

- Wash every dish I use every single time?

- Say yes to that extra PTA commitment?

Instead of defaulting to "everything is urgent," pause and prioritize. For example, you can ask:

- What are my goals for the week?

- What are the must-dos on my to-do list?

- What are the true benefits if I complete _____, _____, and _____ ?

The goal is to optimize your time more efficiently. If you're doing tasks just to check them off a list, you're likely wasting energy that could go toward things that truly matter. By focusing on high-priority items, you create space for the things that bring you joy and meaning.

The Golden Ones and the Drainers

Let's talk about time—specifically, how we waste it. When I consider all the unimportant things that have eaten up my time, it's disheartening. How often have you made yourself available to people and things that don't deserve your time? Maybe it's a friend who constantly drains you, or a project you felt guilted into taking on. Maybe you spend too much time mindlessly scrolling on social media instead of recharging through self-care activities. I once had a friend who constantly called to vent about her life but never asked about mine. At first, I felt obligated to listen, but after a while, I noticed that these conversations left me feeling drained. One day, I decided to set a boundary. I gently told her I couldn't talk during family time. It wasn't an easy conversation, but it freed up my energy to focus on my own needs and my kids.

I've noticed there are two main categories of people, and the quicker you learn who falls into which one, the happier you'll be. The Golden Ones are the people who truly value you. They express gratitude, offer authentic connection, and uplift you. Keep these people close. The Drainers are the ones who take and take, leaving you feeling empty. Recognize these patterns and set boundaries. You can't keep all the energy vampires out of your life, but you can limit their time with you. After a while, they will find other people to latch on to. Stay with the people who will add value to your life and truly support you and your family.

Your time is sacred, and not everyone deserves it. Watch how people respond to your kindness and effort. Do they show gratitude? Respect? Or are they simply taking without giving? When you serve others, do so wholeheartedly, but pay attention to who values your time and effort. Some people will leave you feeling appreciated. Others will drain you. Remember, you're teaching your children how to value themselves and their time by modeling it yourself.

The Power of Compassion

My good friend Susan shared her experience with me, and it highlights how our past struggles shape our ability to empathize. She worked long shifts with no help from family and found it a struggle to juggle everything alone while raising her kids. When she saw other moms with family support, she couldn't relate. Resentment built up because she felt like no one understood how hard it was. "I wanted to give up," she said. "I wanted to quit everything."

Susan's story echoes what so many moms feel: Unsupported. Unseen. Overwhelmed. But what she *did* have was an understanding for other moms who shared her difficulties and the ability to relate to them in a special way. Our struggles shape our compassion. Susan eventually surrounded herself with likeminded women who gave support to one another when it didn't come to them in the traditional ways other moms experienced.

Compassion is a superpower, but different life experiences affect how we access it. When you feel like you have had to do it all yourself, it's hard to find empathy for others who seem to have it easier. And that's okay. Your experience is valid. But here's the twist: While it's okay to have moments of frustration or resentment, those feelings can hold you back. You deserve compassion, so offer it to yourself and to others who need it.

It's Okay to Mess Up

One of the best lessons I've learned from being part of mom communities is this: *Nobody has it all together.* In fact, many moms feel judged for not having it all together. We all spill the formula, forget the diapers, or show up late to practice. And guess what? It's okay. You're human. Our kids will also mess up. They'll have tantrums, struggle with homework, make poor decisions, and test every ounce of patience we have. None of this makes you a bad mom. When we hold ourselves to impossible standards, we let society's obsession with perfection rob us of our joy. Social media doesn't help, as we're constantly comparing our rough drafts to someone else's highlight reel. No one is fault-free. Those who claim perfection are often the furthest from it.

Don't let the scalding opinions of others hold you hostage. The less you care about others' judgement, the freer you'll feel. If your child had a tantrum one day at school and disrupted the class, then understand it was tough day at school. No one should make you feel like a bad mom for your child's tantrums.

I often hear moms ask, "What did I do wrong? Am I a bad mom?" Every time I hear these words, it breaks my heart. The world today is more challenging than ever—overflowing with distractions, endless temptations, and toxic relationships. To make matters worse, we're surrounded by a culture obsessed with unattainable perfection, plastered all over social media. When we're bombarded with these unrealistic ideals, it's easy to feel inadequate, uneasy, and even worthless. But comparison isn't the path to balance and happiness. Yes, we all make mistakes. What matters is how we respond to those moments. Each misstep is an opportunity, a chance to show resilience, to rise above judgement, gossip, and toxicity. Don't let the world's pointed stares or whispered criticisms define you. Instead, let those moments strengthen your authenticity.

When mistakes happen, view them as opportunities to learn and grow, to teach your kids resilience and humility, and to rise above judgement and negativity. When you approach life with this mindset, you will find that every challenge strengthens your sense of self. You'll worry less about outside opinions and more about living a life that aligns with your values.

REFLECTIONS

The Reset Table

Reflection Point	Takeaway	Action Step
Prioritize Tasks	Not everything is urgent. Focus on what truly matters.	Write down three must-dos for the week, and let go of low-priority tasks.
Set Boundaries	Some people and tasks drain your energy. Redistribute your time wisely.	Identify one person or activity that drains you, and set a clear boundary with them this week.
Forgive Mistakes	Mistakes are part of being human. They don't define you.	Reflect on a recent mistake, then reframe it as a learning experience.

TAKEAWAYS

● *Give yourself grace:* Cutting yourself slack means you value your mental and emotional well-being.

● *Prioritize what matters:* When you focus on the essentials, you preserve energy for what truly counts.

● *Set strong boundaries:* Saying no is a powerful yes to yourself and to your peace.

● *Embrace your flaws:* Your imperfections are part of your story. Own them with confidence.

● *Model self-love:* Every time you show yourself compassion, you teach your children to do the same.

● *Release judgment:* Let go of harsh inner criticism and replace it with encouragement. That's how transformation begins.

Chapter Six

Flushing Out Mom Guilt

People very often say to me, "How did you do it? How did you raise a baby and write a book?" And the answer is, I didn't do housework for four years. I am not Superwoman. And living in squalor, that was the answer.
—J.K. Rowling

Mom guilt is relentless. It doesn't matter how much we do, how many sacrifices we make, or how hard we try, there is always that nagging voice whispering, *It's not enough.* It creeps in when the house is a mess, when the kids act out, when dinner isn't made with organic ingredients, when work pulls us away, when exhaustion takes over and we snap at the people we love most. It lingers in the quiet moments and strikes hardest when we least expect it.

I remember scrolling through an online mom group late one night, reading post after post from women drowning in guilt—guilt over daycare drop-offs, missed bedtime stories, fast-food dinners, lost tempers, forgotten school forms. These weren't "bad moms." They were warriors doing their absolute best, yet they still felt like failures.

Why? Because modern motherhood is an impossible equation. We're expected to be everything—career-driven, nurturing, patient, fit, fashionable, available 24/7, emotionally stable, and somehow, still have time for self-care. It's a setup. The guilt is inevitable. But here's what they don't tell you: The level of guilt you feel is not a measure of your love.

A Different Time, a Different Village

Motherhood wasn't always such a guilt-inducing venture. I think back to my own childhood, running wild with my cousins, spending holidays at my aunts' homes, constantly surrounded by family. Back then, motherhood was a shared effort. There were extra hands (grandparents, aunts, neighbors) helping raise the next generation. No one expected a mother to do it alone.

Now? We glorify the Supermom image—the woman who balances work, kids, marriage, home, and personal growth without breaking a sweat. But that's a fantasy. Real moms are often drowning, not thriving. And the guilt? It's a weight we were never meant to carry alone.

Guilt Is Filth

Guilt is like mud. It sticks to you, weighs you down, and gets everywhere if you let it. But it's not permanent. You wouldn't walk around covered in dirt and call it normal, right? No, you'd wash it off. Mom guilt is the same. It's grime you don't need. It doesn't make you a better mom. It doesn't prove your love. It just clogs up your joy and keeps you stuck. Crush it. Wipe it off. Move forward.

Who made these rules? There is no trophy for burnout. No award for suffering in silence. Trying to meet impossible expectations only makes you a miserable mom. The best thing you can do for your children is let go of the need to be perfect and focus on being present. That's what they will remember. Not the spotless house or the perfectly packed lunches, but the love, the laughter, and the way you made them feel safe.

When you're consumed by guilt, you shrink. You apologize for your needs, minimize your dreams, and withhold joy until you've "earned it." Flushing it out means reclaiming your space not just as a mother, but as a whole woman. Because a whole woman raises children who learn how to be whole too.

Moms feel guilty for everything, but nothing weighs heavier than the guilt of self-care. Tell me if this sounds familiar:

- *You finally take an hour to yourself,* but the whole time you're thinking about what you "should" be doing.

- *You feel selfish for getting your nails done,* reading a book, or simply drinking coffee alone.

- *You can't even lock the bathroom door without a small voice yelling,* "Mommy!" and feeling like you have to hurry up and finish.

You can't pour from an empty cup. If you run yourself into the ground, your kids won't get the best version of you; they will get the exhausted, burnt-out, resentful version. And they deserve better than that. You deserve better than that too.

Guilt over Past Mistakes

As moms, we all have moments that haunt us. Maybe it was snapping at your child when you were exhausted. Maybe it was missing a school event. Maybe it was struggling with patience when they needed you to be calm. Motherhood is messy. It's full of mistakes. But what defines you isn't the moment you wish you could take back; it's how you show up the next time. Your child doesn't need a perfect mom. They need a loving, human mom. One who tries, who learns, who apologizes when necessary, and who keeps showing up.

I was raised by a mother who worked her fingers to the bone to provide for us. Her work ethic was relentless. She didn't have time for guilt. She had bills to pay, mouths to feed, and a future to build for her children. As a kid, I didn't fully grasp what she was carrying. I saw her strength, but I didn't see the nights she went to bed anxious, the exhaustion that clung to her bones, the quiet sacrifices she made every day.

Now that I'm a mom, I see it. And I know so many of you feel that same weight—the never-ending bills, the stress of making ends meet, the pressure to create a better future for your kids. Your children may not understand your sacrifices now, but one day they will. And when they do, they'll carry your strength with them.

Guilt Does Not Equal Love

Motherhood is not meant to be a martyrdom. It's part of your unfolding. Flushing out the guilt allows you to integrate all the parts of you: mother, woman, soul, dreamer, creator. And when you give yourself that permission, you give your children a living example of how to carry their own roles in life with grace, freedom, and self-trust, preparing them to take center stage one day like you!

Guilt exists because we love our children fiercely. But instead of letting it weigh us down, let's flip the script. Instead of saying, "I feel guilty for working late," say, "I'm proud that I'm providing for my family." Instead of saying, "I feel guilty for taking time for myself," say, "I'm teaching my kids that self-care is important." Guilt doesn't make us better moms. Love does.

Mom guilt is real, but it doesn't have to run your life. Let's flush it for good.

REFLECTIONS

Releasing Mom Guilt

Prompt	Reflection	Example Response
Identify the source of your guilt.	"I feel guilty because _____."	"I feel guilty because I missed my child's school performance."
Challenge the guilt.	"Is this guilt based on realistic expectations or unrealistic ideals?"	"It's unrealistic. I can't always control my work schedule."
Rewrite the narrative.	"Instead of feeling guilty, I can acknowledge _____."	"Instead of feeling guilty, I can acknowledge I'm doing my best."
Celebrate a recent success.	"One way I showed love or care for my child this week was _____."	"I cooked their favorite dinner and helped with homework."

Action Steps to Release Mom Guilt

1. Create a "guilt filter." Before you let guilt in, ask:

- Is this realistic?

- Would I judge another mom for this?

- Will this matter in five years?

2. Celebrate small wins. Each week, write down one thing you did well as a mom.

3. Replace negative self-talk with an affirmation.

- *I am doing enough.*

- *My love is enough.*

- *I am a great mom, even on hard days.*

TAKEAWAYS

- *Guilt is a trap.* It keeps you stuck in shame instead of moving forward.

- *Perfection is a lie.* You don't have to "do it all" to be a good mom.

- *Your love is enough.* Your kids won't remember flawless. They will remember feeling loved.

- *You deserve joy too.* Take care of yourself without apology.

- *You're not alone.* Every mom feels guilt at some point. Sharing your truth builds connection and reminds others they're not the only ones struggling.

- *Presence beats perfection.* What your child needs most is your attention, not your performance.

- *Release to rise.* Letting go of guilt makes space for joy, clarity, and self-trust.

Chapter Seven

Stop Self-Sabotaging

You've been berating yourself for years with no results. See
what happens if you attempt to approve of yourself.
—Louise Hay

People's opinions can be damning, but nothing compares
to the war we wage inside our own minds. The constant
self-doubt, the guilt, the mental beatdowns. We proudly
call it "being responsible," "putting others first," or "doing
the right thing." In reality, we're sabotaging ourselves.
Moms, we are professionals at powering through. We
could be running on fumes, barely holding it together, but
if someone needs us, what do we do without question? We
show up. And that sounds noble, until you realize we're
the ones we never show up for.

I've been there. Ignoring my exhaustion. Silencing my needs. Pouring from an empty cup and calling it love. But sacrificing ourselves on the altar of motherhood only burns us out, making us feel resentful and lost. At some point, we have to ask ourselves: *When does this cycle end?*

The Martyr Mom Myth

I once saw a Facebook post that read "Pay attention to the moms who never have their hair or nails done. They're the ones doing right by their kids." And the comments poured in, praising these moms as if sacrificing their happiness, health, and identity was the ultimate badge of honor. When did we decide that self-neglect is a virtue? That a mom's worth is measured by how much of herself she gives up? I have friends who live this reality—working tirelessly, always putting themselves last. They do it out of love, but the toll it takes is undeniable. The truth? Self-sacrifice is neither sustainable nor honorable.

The Boredom Battle

Here's a relatable scene: Your child flops onto the couch, sighing dramatically, "Mom, I'm bored." Your first instinct? Fix it. Entertain them. Find something fun to do. Because isn't that what good moms do? Wrong. Their boredom isn't your problem to fix. Boredom is their doorway to creativity. When kids aren't being constantly entertained or directed, they will look around and do something with what they have. That's where imagination kicks in. A stick becomes a sword. A cardboard box becomes a spaceship. A blank afternoon leads to a new idea.

Growing up, I had plenty of boredom moments. I'd wander outside, twirling in my mother's rose garden, plucking petals (which I'm sure she wasn't thrilled about). I'd write poems, stare at the sky, dream about my future. I didn't need my mom to schedule my every moment.

Somewhere along the way, boredom became a problem to solve, and moms became the fixers. Boredom is not the enemy. It's the entry point to discovering something new. Kids do not need their parents supplying constant entertainment. They need space to develop, explore, problem-solve, and test ideas. If we always swoop in with *our* ideas, they will never learn to handle their own restlessness and create.

If we constantly entertain our kids, we teach them to rely on us for their happiness while draining ourselves dry. Next time your child complains, try this: "Boredom is where great ideas are born. Go find one." Don't sabotage your energy by taking away opportunities for your kids to grow and lean into their independence.

The Price of Self-Neglect

Mom, you deserve to thrive. You cannot flourish if you are exhausted, constantly putting yourself last. Your burnout ripples into your home, your relationships, your children. Would you want your children to live in a constant state of self-neglect? No? Then why are you allowing it for yourself? Set an example and break the cycle.

Self-sabotage is sneaky. It often shows up disguised as something honorable:

- Being a yes woman because you don't want to disappoint anyone.

- Procrastinating personal goals because you feel guilty focusing on yourself.

- Comparing yourself to other moms.

When that annoying voice pops into your mind saying, *You're a terrible mom,* or *You're being selfish,* pause and ask yourself: Is this inner voice one that is helping me or harming me?

One of the best tools I've found for overcoming negative self-talk is Shad Helmstetter's book, *What to Say When You Talk to Yourself.* The way we speak to and about ourselves matters; language shapes our reality. For instance, instead of saying, "I have no time for myself because my kids need me," try saying, "Taking care of myself makes me a better mom." Our words matter. Use them wisely.

The Litmus Test of No

A great way to gauge whether you're sabotaging yourself is to examine how often you say no.

- Do you say no to your kids when requests are unreasonable or when fulfilling them would exhaust you?

- Do you say no to opportunities or ideas because you're afraid of failing or because you doubt your abilities?

- How often do you tell yourself no when considering something you *want*—whether it's time to rest, a personal indulgence, or pursuing a long-buried dream?

Learning to say no to the right things (and yes to yourself) takes practice. It starts with small steps, like recognizing when your energy reserves are low and giving yourself permission to catch up on rest. It grows into bigger decisions, like pursuing a new career or a creative project that ignites your passion.

The point isn't to say no all the time but to stop letting guilt, fear, or the pressure to be everything to everyone else dictate your decisions. When you begin to set boundaries, you'll discover something phenomenal: The world keeps moving, and your loved ones will adjust.

Instead of beating yourself up for not being perfect, overextending yourself to prove you are "enough," and silencing your own needs for the sake of others, speak to yourself kindly, like you would your best friend. Prioritize yourself (drink water, go for a walk, take five minutes to breathe). Pursue something that lights you up (a hobby, a passion, a career move).

A thriving mom is empowered, not perfect.

REFLECTIONS

Stop Self-Sabotaging

1. *Identity your Patterns:*

● List three ways you tend to self-sabotage (overextending yourself, speaking negatively to yourself, neglecting your health). *Example: I always say yes to things even when I'm exhausted.*

Self-sabotage #1

_____

_____

Self-sabotage #2

_____

_____

Self-sabotage #3

_____

_____

2. *Recognize Triggers*

● What situations or feelings tend to trigger self-sabotage patterns? *Example: I feel guilty saying no to my kids or when I'm criticized by others.*

My Triggers:

_____

_____

3. Reframe Negative Thoughts:

● Write down one self-deprecating thought you often have, then rewrite it as an empowering thought. *Example: (negative) "I'm not good enough to be an author." (positive) "I am capable and willing to learn."*

My Thoughts

Negative

_____

_____

Positive

_____

_____

● Think of a recent situation where you said no to something. Was it your kids, yourself, or an opportunity? *Example: "I said no to myself when I skipped going to the gym because I felt guilty leaving my family."*

Your Example:

_____

_____

_____

_____

● How could you have approached the situation differently? Rewrite the circumstance with a self-supportive outcome. *Example: "Instead of skipping the gym, I could have gone for thirty minutes and then spent time with my family."*

Your Rewrite

_____

_____

_____

_____

TAKEAWAYS

- *Awareness is key.* You can't change what you don't recognize.

- *Saying no = saying yes to yourself.* Boundaries protect your well-being.

- *Small steps lead to big shifts.* Even tiny changes make a difference.

- *You deserve self-love.* The more you care for yourself, the better you can show up for others.

- *Stop self-sabotaging.* Say yes to yourself. The moment you do, you'll unlock new dimensions of yourself.

- *Create a self-care ritual.* Pick one small way to prioritize yourself daily.

Chapter Eight

Routines = Sanity

These were her rituals, the routines that made her feel alive and connected. Without them, where would she be? Lost.

—Ben Sherwood

What if the chaos in your life could be tamed not by grand gestures but by simple, consistent routines? Imagine waking up each day knowing exactly what steps to take to bring calm and order to your life. Routines may not sound glamorous, but they are the unsung heroes of our sanity. When life feels overwhelming, routines anchor us. They create rhythm, a predictable flow that allows us to thrive amid the storms of daily life. Without them, we're like a ship with no captain, aimlessly drifting. With them, we navigate toward peace and purpose.

When your days have rhythm, your mind has space. You stop wasting energy on constant decision-making and start investing it in things that matter. Routines become reliable patterns when your life feels chaotic and unpredictable. They also help you build self-trust. Every time you engage in a routine, you send a powerful message: *I can count on me.* That sense of trust is the bedrock of confidence, allowing you to take center stage of your life. On a neurological level, routines soothe the nervous system and make us feel safe, acting as form of medicine—simple, steady, and healing. Don't let your routine become inflexible though. If you feel you must do things in a certain way "or else," then it's time to let go instead of it running your life. Overall, having a routine helps you synch your mind and body to a predictable rhythm, no matter how hectic life becomes.

The Psychology of Routine

There's a reason routines feel like a lifeline when everything else feels chaotic. They act as emotional stabilizers. Our brains crave rhythm and predictability. It's why toddlers melt down when naptime shifts and why we, as adults, feel off when we skip a morning ritual or lose track of our day.

Routines give your nervous system a place to rest. They quiet decision fatigue by removing some of the guesswork. You no longer have to wonder, *What should I do next?* because your rhythm is already holding that space for you. That matters when you're carrying the invisible weight of motherhood—mentally managing schedules, planning meals, running the household, and tending to everyone's emotional needs all at once.

A good routine is anchoring. It doesn't trap you in perfectionism but frees you from overwhelm. It's not about doing the same thing at the same time every day like a robot. It's about returning to your rhythm in the midst of a busy life. Your routine is your reset.

Growing up in Guyana, life was simple. We didn't own a car. I didn't even have a bicycle! I didn't crave either of those things because I had what I needed, and that was enough. It was a humble life, and matters such as fueling a vehicle were nowhere on my radar. So when I got married in America and started taking road trips with my husband, he would often get frustrated: "The car doesn't have gas!" It wasn't that I was careless. I had just never developed the habit of thinking about fuel. I had to learn (through a few bumpy starts) that a smooth trip required preparation.

Now I have a system. When I'm getting ready to go anywhere, it's automatic. I can practically close my eyes and get it all done—bags packed, gas in the car, everything prepped. Systems like that turn my chaos into calm. Without a routine, you'll find yourself rushing out the door at the last minute, scrambling to find your outfit, printing documents, and leaving the house frazzled. When you prepare, the day goes smoother.

Not every area of your life needs a system, but the parts that do will benefit immensely. A good system of operation will offset struggles with time management and help your day to flow seamlessly.

For example:

- *Morning Routine*: Wake up, meditate for five minutes, exercise, and review your to-do list.

- *Work Prep*: Lay out your clothes, pack a lunch, and prep materials the night before.

- *Meal Planning*: Create a weekly menu to save time and reduce decision fatigue.

Routines free you to focus on what truly matters.

Deliberate Practice

Deliberate practices are the intentional habits that set the tone for your day. For me, one of these practices is affirmations. Every morning, as soon as I put my car in drive, my kids and I recite affirmations together. It's become a ritual we all look forward to—a grounding moment before the chaos of the day. Another deliberate practice is writing. I carve out specific hours in the day to write, and I stick to them. Of course, life happens, and I sometimes miss a session. The key is not to quit; simply rest and restart.

Life isn't perfect, and neither are we. What separates those who succeed from those who don't is the ability to adapt. If a forty-five-minute meditation feels overwhelming, shorten it to five minutes. If an hour-long workout feels impossible, break it into two ten-minute sessions. The goal is consistency. Find what works for you, and make it part of your life.

REFLECTIONS

• *Audit Your Day*: Identify one area of your life that feels chaotic and then brainstorm a simple system to bring order. *Example: Create a morning checklist to streamline your routine.*

• *Choose a Deliberate Practice*: Start small. Commit to one new habit this week and track your progress.

• *Example: Spend five minutes every evening reflecting on what went well that day.*

• *Simplify Your Tools*: Decide if you prefer a digital or physical planner, and then commit to using one method consistently.

• *Example: Buy a new calendar and colored pens and create activities that are color-coded (perfect if you're a visual kind of person). Or download an app that provides digital "rewards" when you tick things off your list.*

INTENTION SETTING

1. Write down three deliberate habits you want to cultivate into a routine. (Example: Exercise for ten minutes, start a gratitude journal, or prep meals for the week.)

_____

_____

_____

TAKEAWAYS

• *Routines equal stability*: A consistent routine can bring peace and order, even in the busiest seasons of life.

• *Systems simplify life*: Create systems that support your success and reduce unnecessary stress.

• *Deliberate practices create transformation over time*: Small, intentional habits compound over time into significant life changes.

• *Adapt, don't quit*: Adjust your routines and habits as needed, but keep going. Consistency is the key to success.

• *Your routine reflects your priorities*: When you design your day with intention, you're declaring what really matters to you.

Chapter Nine

Functionality

The intentions of a tool are what it does. A hammer intends to strike, a vise intends to hold fast, a lever intends to lift. But sometimes a tool may have other uses that you don't know. Sometimes in doing what you intend, you also do what the knife intends, without knowing.
—Philip Pullman

Some things in life don't need to be so hard, but we make them that way out of habit, nostalgia, or even guilt. We scrub instead of simplify. We grind instead of delegate. We hold on tight when we could be letting something (or someone) help.

Functionality is about clearing space for ease. It's about recognizing that the right tools, the right systems, and the right mindset can transform not only your day but your life. From apps to appliances, rituals to routines, the tools are out there. The question is: Are you using them?

Scrub Steps to Save Time

Growing up in Guyana, life looked very different from the one I live now. My family lived in a humble two-bedroom house no larger than my family room. It stood tall, about fourteen feet on stilts. The walls were unpainted for much of my childhood: bare wood, sans ceiling, a simple zinc roof, wooden windows. That little house was filled with love and warmth. It didn't need painted walls, a ceiling, roof tiles, or any other update to be filled with love. Love was the foundation. But I digress. Having a home like this essentially left our family exposed to the elements. The torrential downpours and the stifling humidity were always present, so we needed to protect and care for our humble home. We needed to protect the bones of our foundation. And that took time and effort.

As a teenager, I took pride in helping my mom, who worked six days a week running her small business. One of my self-assigned jobs was cleaning the fourteen steps that led to our veranda. Armed with a metal scraper, I'd remove the dirt and grime that had accumulated, step by step. It was hard physical work, and by the time I was done, I'd be drenched in sweat.

Another chore was washing clothes by hand. This was mostly done by my mom, but as a child I always strived to ease her workload. I can still picture the classic blue soap we used and the washboard that helped scrub each piece clean. The process was labor-intensive: Fill the tub, soak the clothes, scrub, rinse, and hang everything on the line. In the humid heat of Guyana, this task was an all-day affair.

Fast-forward to today, and those same tasks take a fraction of the time. I still marvel at my washing machine every time I load it. Yet I notice that even with all the modern conveniences, we sometimes cling to outdated methods of doing things out of guilt or pride. We tell ourselves we need to do it all, even when help is right there in front of us.

Add a Personal Touch

Not every task needs to be outsourced. Some things (like gardening) hold a therapeutic charm for me. On my patio, I have a small garden box where I grow basil, turmeric, mint, scallions, and other herbs. It's good for the environment, good for my health, and good for my soul.

But for other tasks—like vacuuming under the beds—I gladly let my iRobot do the heavy lifting. Maybe you love organizing your closets every year, or crafting cards for loved ones' special days, or cooking an elaborate meal every weekend instead of going to a restaurant. The key is balance. Ask yourself: *What can I delegate to tools, systems, or people? And what do I want to keep as part of my life because it brings me joy?*

Create Order

Functionality thrives in an environment of order. A life of chaos (in your personal environment or your mind) makes it nearly impossible to live productively. Imagine trying to cook dinner in a kitchen where the sink is full, the counters are cluttered, and the stove is dirty. Just looking at the mess can drain your energy and derail the attempt to even start the task. When my kids were little, managing the home always felt like a juggling act. The constant cooking, cleaning, and organizing never seemed to end.

Over the years, I have leaned into streamlining order in my life, and it's so worth it! Creating order doesn't have to be overwhelming. Start small: Tidy one drawer. Set a fifteen-minute timer and tackle a single task from start to finish. Use tools like checklists, planners, or timers to stay on track. For me, creating order starts with an action plan. Take Thanksgiving, for example. Every year, my family gathers at our home, and I start planning weeks in advance. From menu planning to grocery shopping to assigning tasks, every detail is mapped out. This level of preparation turns a potentially chaotic event into a jubilant, seamless experience. When you give yourself a roadmap, you create clarity and flow, which is the foundation of functionality.

The Power of Preparation

Preparation isn't glamorous, but it is life-changing. It saves time, reduces stress, and even saves money. For years, I struggled with letting food spoil in the fridge— fresh vegetables bought with good intentions but never used in time. To fix this, I've developed a simple system. When I come home from the store, I wash, chop, and label my vegetables right away. If I know I won't use something immediately, I freeze it. This simple habit has transformed how I cook. It eliminates waste and allows me to whip up healthy meals quickly. Meal-planning is another game-changer. Using my Notes app, I create a monthly dinner menu. It's not rigid but provides structure. Knowing what's for dinner reduces decision fatigue and keeps me on track with my health and budget goals.

Tech Tips

We live in the Information Age, and the tools at our fingertips are extraordinary. From productivity apps to smart calendars, these simple tools can revolutionize your daily life if you let them.

For example:

- *The Notes App*: Use it to create checklists, scan receipts, create PDF documents, and even lock sensitive information.

- *Digital Calendars*: Schedule events with reminders, add locations, determine travel times, color-code events by category, and share with family members.

- *Timers*: Use them to stay focused on tasks or manage your time effectively throughout the day.

These tools serve as allies in creating a life that flows. The question is, are you using them to their full potential?

Habit Stacking

The concept of habit stacking is simple but effective: You attach a new habit to an existing one, creating a natural flow that builds momentum. The existing habit serves as a trigger for the new one, making it easier to integrate into your routine.

Here are some examples of habit stacking:

- While brewing your morning coffee, write down your top three priorities for the day.

- While brushing your teeth, listen to a motivational podcast or audiobook.

- Before sitting down to dinner, take five minutes to tidy up the living room with your family.

When I started building better habits, I paired them with things I was already doing daily. For instance, every time I load the dishwasher, I wipe down the countertops. It takes less than five extra minutes, but it keeps my kitchen feeling fresh and functional. Start small. Don't try to stack too many habits at once. Focus on one or two, and once they feel natural, add more.

Automation

Automation is a form of self-preservation, not just convenience. Every day, we make hundreds of decisions, from what to wear to what to cook. That constant decision-making drains us. That's where automation steps in, like a quiet assistant clearing the mental clutter and giving us back our bandwidth. Having some things automated allows you to make fewer micro-decisions so you can focus your energy on what actually matters: your family, your health, your passions, your peace. Here are some things I find helpful to automate:

1. *Household tasks*: Let technology carry the load. My robot vacuum glides under beds and sofas while I'm doing other things, like working, spending time with my kids, or sipping a cup of tea.

2. *Meal prep and groceries*: Set up recurring grocery deliveries, or try a meal kit service to remove the weekly mental gymnastics. Batch-cook and freeze meals on weekends. It's like sending a gift to your future self.

3. *Finances*: Automate your bill payments. It saves you from last-minute stress and late fees. Use budgeting apps like Mint or YNAB to track spending and make informed choices without having to rethink everything month to month.

4. *Health and wellness*: Let a smart water bottle track your hydration. Use fitness apps that design your workouts and remind you to move. Show up where it matters and you'll have the energy to expend in all the important places.

5. *Family coordination*: Shared digital calendars (like Google Calendar or iCalendar) can keep your whole household in sync. Set recurring reminders for birthdays, family game nights, and even self-care moments.

I used to forget to send birthday wishes to friends (and some family!) until I started adding them to my calendar with yearly reminders. Now I not only remember to send a quick "happy birthday" text, I actually show up for my loved ones with intention. That one change deepened my relationships and relieved me of unnecessary guilt. That's the power of automation.

The Turning Point

I remember a season when everything felt like it was slipping through the cracks. I was juggling work, parenting, and trying to keep the house in decent order. But every day felt like I was sprinting behind a train I could never catch. One night I was feeling particularly overwhelmed. The house was a mess, dinner wasn't planned, and the kids needed help with homework. I sat at the kitchen table and stared at the clutter, feeling paralyzed to take any action. That night, I promised myself I would stop doing things the hard way just because I thought I had to. I started small by setting up auto-pay, creating recurring reminders, and planning weekly meals. Little by little, the chaos quieted. Not overnight, but enough that I could breathe again.

At its core, functionality is about doing what matters most and creating space for the life you want to live, free from unnecessary stress and chaos. When we embrace tools and habits that support our goals, we free ourselves to focus on what truly matters: our health, our relationships, and our passions. So start small. Pick one tool, one habit, or one task, and commit to making it more streamlined. Because the easier life flows, the more energy you'll have to focus on what really matters: *you.*

REFLECTIONS

The true power of functionality lies in how it shows up in everyday moments. It allows you to focus on living with intention. These reflection prompts are designed to help you pause and take inventory of what's working, what's not, and where small shifts can create a big impact. As you read through them, remember that the goal is progress, not perfection. Pick one area that speaks to you, and let that be your starting point toward a life that flows with more ease and purpose.

1. *Habit Reflection:*

   • What is one habit you already do daily that you could pair with a new habit? *(Example: While driving to appointments, listen to a podcast or an audio book.)*

2. *Functional Order:*

   • Is there an area in your home that causes stress or inefficiency? How could you reorganize it to make life easier? *(Example: Clear your kitchen counters to make cooking feel less chaotic.)*

3. *Automation Ideas:*

● What is one repetitive task you could automate this week? *(Example: Schedule recurring reminders for birthdays, or set up auto-pay for bills.)*

4. *Preparation Insights:*

● What is one thing you could prepare in advance to reduce stress later? *(Example: Create a grab-and-go section in your fridge for prepped meals and snacks.)*

5. *Tool Exploration:*

● What is one tool or gadget you've been curious about but haven't tried? *(Example: Use a meal prep app or robot vacuum to free up more time so you can focus on your family or passions.)*

TAKEAWAYS:

Lessons on Functionality

• *Small changes add up*: One small improvement (like automating a bill or preparing veggies ahead of time) can reduce stress and free up your energy.

• *Pair habits for success*: Stacking new habits onto existing ones builds momentum without feeling overwhelmed.

• *Preparation saves time and energy*: Prepping ahead of time reduces decision fatigue.

• *Embrace tools and technology*: Don't shy away from innovations that can simplify your life and maximize your time.

• *Order promotes flow*: A tidy, organized space fosters mental clarity and increases productivity.

Chapter Ten

Reject Me, Please!

While rejection is a possibility—an inevitable fact of life—the greatest rejection lies in denying yourself the opportunity by opting not to pursue it at all.
—Erwin D. Maramat

Rejection. It's a heavy word, isn't it? It can bruise our egos, dismantle our self-worth, and make us question our dreams. Whether it's chasing a lifelong goal or facing setbacks in relationships, rejection stings. But what if we saw rejection not as an enemy but as a teacher? The truth is, the more rejection we face, the stronger we become. Each no is an opportunity to grow, refine, and persevere. No one welcomes rejection, but it can be the catalyst for our most significant breakthroughs.

Take my journey, for example. As a little girl, I dreamed of a bigger life, though it felt impossibly far away. My biological father passed away when I was just four years old. By all accounts—from the few tender memories I carry—he was a kind, compassionate man, a natural leader, and a devoted father. Losing him at such a young age left a hole in our family and in my understanding of what life was supposed to look like. For a long time, I couldn't help but wonder, *Why me? Why us?*

My mom became a widow in a third-world country with two young children to raise and no partner to share the burden with. In a culture where being a woman already came with limitations, being a widowed woman meant even fewer options. She had no financial safety net, and certainly no reprieve. With the support of her siblings and our extended family, she carried everything—our needs, our futures—on her back.

When I was thirteen, everything changed. My mom married a wonderful man who would come to be my dad in every way that mattered. He embraced all of us with humility and an open heart that changed the trajectory of our lives. I remember how his family folded us in as their own, how there was no distinction between "his family" and "her family." We became a united front, and that model of unconditional love and quiet strength has stayed with me ever since.

But it wasn't easy. My dad made enormous sacrifices to help us come to America. He worked long days in Manhattan as a security guard, waking up at 4:30 a.m. Bananas and milk were often his go-to meal—simple and affordable, a small act of discipline to stretch every dollar. He sent money home, always putting our future ahead of his own comfort. I carry that image with me—the image of a man giving up rest, ease, and even the smallest luxuries for a future he might never fully enjoy himself. That's what love and determination looked like to me. And I will never forget that for as long as I live.

So when I finally stepped onto the bustling streets of New York City in 2003 at the age of seventeen, it was a hard-won victory. That dream I'd envisioned while twirling barefoot in my garden back in Guyana? It came true because of sacrifice, resilence, and the unwavering belief that I was meant for more. When I feel like giving up, I remember that story. I remember my dads—both my heavenly and earthly father. And I remember that sometimes, the greatest strength isn't in what we say, but in what we're willing to endure for those we love.

The Choice to Persevere

Rejection can either make us bitter or better. The choice is ours. We can wallow in self-pity, letting rejection define us, or we can choose to see it as a stepping stone. History shows us that anyone who has accomplished something remarkable has faced rejection.

My cousin Indira is a living example of resilience. Born with a severe physical disability, she grew up crawling on her knees and relying on a wheelchair. Life handed her countless challenges and rejections, but she never let them deter her. Her defeats were never claimed as setbacks. It was just another reason to forge forward. I'm in awe of her willpower, her discipline, and her ability to overcome the challenges of life.

Today, Indira is married, owns a home, and runs a small business. She even drives an electric bike! She is active in her community, sitting on boards, helping those in need, and inspiring everyone around her. Her victories are monumental because she chose to overcome instead of giving up. How many of us have every physical ability and opportunity yet still hold ourselves back?

The Beauty in Struggles

The struggles we face aren't our enemies; they're the canvases upon which we paint our victories. Each rejection, failure, or setback has the potential to shape us into stronger, more capable versions of ourselves. Aishwarya Rai Bachchan is one of my favorite actresses. She performed an intricate dance in the Bollywood movie *Hum Dil De Chuke Sanam*. I later learned that during the rehearsals, she bruised her knees and feet but never complained. If you saw her epic dance sliding on her knees and sailing elegantly in the air, you'd be in awe of her too. Needless to say, her perseverance brought the world an unforgettable performance. The same principle applies to our lives. We may stumble, our spirits may become crushed, but those moments of discomfort often lead to our most profound growth. The way I see it, we can either dwell in that defeated place, or we can remain determined, able to see the bigger picture unfolding.

Rejection Leads to Teachable Moments

Rejection serves as a teacher, providing feedback and insight that we are often blind to. It chisels us, sharpens our skills, and teaches us patience and resilience—but only if we're willing to reflect. When I first moved to Florida, I didn't know how to drive. Determined, I walked to the store in the blazing sun, carrying heavy bags with sweaty hands. Eventually, that became too burdensome, so I finally took driving lessons. When I went for my test, guess what happened? I hit the curb and failed. After that experience, I became determined to pass because my goal was to attend college, so I practiced every day in an empty parking lot. The next time I took the test, I passed. That simple experience taught me two things: Rejection isn't permanent, and persistence always pays off.

Empty Pages

Imagine your life as a book. What would it look like if every page were empty? If every challenge had been smoothed out for you? The victories we cherish are meaningful because they require grit. They require us to take risks, fail, and try again. So, what will you dare to do? Will you start that business? Write that book? Go back to school? Yes, rejection may be part of the journey, but don't let the fear of what might happen hold you back.

The Lesson in No

Rejection isn't always about you. Sometimes it's about timing. Other times, it's about fit. But often, it's an opportunity to get better. When I failed my first driving test, the problem wasn't the test; it was my lack of preparation. I needed to spend more time behind the wheel, practicing, learning, and growing. When I finally passed, it was because I had grown in confidence through discipline.

Every no is a chance to polish your edges. It's a reminder that we don't need to stay stuck in defeat; we can refine our skills, reevaluate our approach, and come back stronger. Rejection asks us to dig deeper, to refine our craft, and to push beyond our limits. It forces us to ask hard questions, face uncomfortable truths, and in doing so, it helps us grow.

The Refining Fire

Gold is purified in fire, and so are we. Rejection is like that fire. Yes, it hurts, but it also transforms. It burns away insecurity, polishes our potential, and builds endurance. The key is perspective. Instead of asking, "Why me?" ask, "What is this teaching me?"

I remember a season when this refining process was especially personal. When my eldest son was very young, my husband and I were building a network marketing business. It demanded more than just our time; it required travel, leadership, and endless hours of planning and presenting. We led a team of hundreds, often hosting events and training sessions that pushed me far beyond my comfort zone. There were lots of meetings— sometimes multiple per day and on the weekends! It required speaking on a whim, creating presentations, and solving problems in real time. I quickly recognized these were life skills, and they were shaping me.

It wasn't easy. There were times I had to leave my son in the care of a sitter or my mother-in-law (who is always willing and helpful), and the guilt of that often clashed with my desire to grow. I wrestled with what it meant to be a "good mom." I questioned whether I was selfish or misguided. But in hindsight, that season refined me. It stretched my communication, deepened my resilience, and taught me how to lead with conviction while nurturing. That business—those challenges—lit a fire in me that still burns today. It wasn't rejection in the traditional sense, but it felt like rejection at times— rejection of comfort, of ease, of the idea that I could "have it all" without sacrifice. And yet, it made me better. Stronger. Clearer on who I was becoming.

A Tool for Strength

Imagine lifting weights. The resistance is what builds muscle. Rejection works the same way. Every no you hear is a repetition that makes you stronger, more determined, and more capable. Let rejection fuel your fire. Let it challenge you to improve, to innovate, and to persevere. And when success finally comes (and it will) it'll be that much sweeter because you will have earned it.

Rejection can feel like darkness, but it's often the shadow cast by the light of success waiting on the other side. To move forward, you must be willing to analyze your failures with honesty and objectivity. What can you do differently? Where can you improve? Most importantly, how can you rise again? The obstacles in your path are there to shape you. So put on your blinders, focus on your goals, and let rejection refine, not define you.

REFLECTIONS

Your Rejection Reset

1. *Recall a recent rejection.*

Think of a time you faced rejection (personal or professional). What happened, and how did it make you feel?

_____

_____

2. *Identify the lesson.*

What did you learn from this experience? How has it strengthened or shaped you?

_____

_____

3. *Shift your perspective.*

What unexpected good came out of it? Did it open a new door or teach you something valuable?

_____

_____

4. *Decide what's next.*

What is one step you can take today to grow, improve, or move forward?

_____

_____

5. *Create your personal rejection mantra.*

When I face rejection, I will remind myself:

_____

_____

Build Your Resilience Toolkit

Exercise	How to Do It
Rejection Journal	Track rejections for one week. Note the lessons and how you'll improve.
Positive Affirmations	Choose a phase to repeat daily. Example: "Every no brings me closer to a yes."
Gratitude Shift	List three things you're grateful for, even in the midst of rejection.
Seek Feedback	Ask a trusted person for insights on how you can grow or pivot.

TAKEAWAYS

● *Rejection is a teacher*: It refines your strengths and chisels away what no longer serves you.

● *Rejection builds endurance*: Each no toughens your resolve and makes the yes sweeter.

● *Perspective is everything*: Reframing rejection transforms it into a stepping stone.

● *Action beats fear*: Progress begins when you act despite the risk of rejection.

● *Your story needs struggle*: Rejection is a powerful chapter, not the conclusion.

Chapter Eleven

Reclaiming Your Mind

You owe yourself the love that you so freely give to other people.
—Unknown

Our minds can often feel like a chaotic traffic jam, polluted with honking worries, backed-up regrets, and a never-ending line of responsibilities. This mental congestion can bring us to a complete halt. *Mind clutter* is the mental overload and unnecessary noise in your head. *Past worries* signal regrets or replaying old conversations. *Future anxiety* focuses on what could go wrong. *The daily overload* is a never-ending to-do list and the pressure to be everything to everyone. *Digital noise* is the constant notifications, emails, and the addictive pull of social media.

This clutter takes up valuable mental real estate, making it harder to focus on what truly matters. It saps our energy, clouds our judgement, and leaves little room for creativity, joy, or peace. Our thoughts can become caged in our minds, swirling the past, present, and future around with no clear escape. But there is a release. The balm for the unseen weight we carry in our minds often comes in the form of writing. There is nothing quite like pouring your thoughts onto a page—tracing the roots of your emotions, understanding where they stem from, and making peace with what once felt unbearable.

When I was a child, I often felt unfortunate. I was blessed with a loving, devoted mother, but what haunted me was the absence of my father. I was just four years old (and my brother was eight) when he passed. Years later, I asked the same aching questions: "Why me? Why us?" When I looked out at the world, all I saw were families with both parents. Joy. Wholeness. What seemed like complete, untouchable happiness.

I used to climb the fifteen-foot scaffold that held our water in huge tanks. It became my thinking spot. My sanctuary. And sometimes, especially when it rained, it became the place where I cried out to the heavens and cursed the life I'd been dealt. I was an angry teen, but I pretended otherwise. I smiled at school, followed the rules, remained polite and composed at home. But a red-hot fury was buried deep beneath the surface, festering like a wound that wouldn't heal.

Then something shifted. I wrote an essay for a regional competition. And to my surprise, I placed second. When I went to collect my prize at the regional office, I saw something in a glass case: a beautiful diary. I wanted one. And when I finally got my own, I poured my heart into it every day. That diary became my release. My clarity. My comfort.

Through writing, my perspective began to change. I still didn't have all the answers about my father's death— maybe I never will—but I began to see the bigger picture. I saw how every hardship, every heartbreak, every silent scream shaped me. Built me. Strengthened me. The painful memories didn't vanish, but they did transform my perspective. But transformation isn't a one-time event. Life kept happening. And somewhere along the way (between motherhood, ambition, and trying to hold it all together) I became tired—physically, mentally, emotionally, and spiritually.

That's the thing about mind clutter. It builds slowly, like a fog. And one day, you wake up and realize you can't see clearly anymore—not your goals, not your joy, not even yourself. That's when I began to ask: *What thoughts am I allowing to stay here rent-free? Which ones are building me up, and which ones are breaking me down?*

Is My Mental Dialogue Serving Me?

At some point, I realized I was being talked to, all day long, by my own mind. And most of the messages weren't kind. They weren't even true. But they had become familiar. Automatic. Some of the thoughts I was silently repeating to myself:

- "You're lagging behind. Everyone else has life figured out."

- "You have to keep pushing or everything will fall apart."

- "Don't stop. You haven't earned rest yet."

- "You should be doing more. Always more."

I thought those thoughts were helping me stay motivated, but all they were really doing was feeding my angst. They kept me spinning, striving, doubting. They filled my mental space with noise, and none of it was peaceful. But slowly, through stillness, I began to hear a different voice. A quieter one. One that reminded me of truths I had forgotten. I had to choose to listen to it. To give it space. To believe it on purpose. Over time, I developed a healthy mental dialogue:

- "You're allowed to slow down."

- "Doing your best is enough."

- "You're not behind—you're exactly where you need to be."

- "You don't have to prove your worth. You already have it."

The shift wasn't instant, but it was powerful. I learned that reclaiming my mind meant challenging the thoughts I had accepted without question. So I started asking:

- Whose voice is this?

- Is this thought helping me or hurting me?

- What would I rather believe instead?

Those questions gave me agency. They helped me replace mental clutter with clarity, and reaction with intention. They helped me reclaim my mind, one belief at a time.

My Tipping Point with Mental Clutter

In 2017, life was moving at a pace that felt impossible to keep up with. We were running an e-commerce business, traveling constantly, and I was juggling demanding clients—some of whom would call me at midnight with "urgent" needs. On top of that, we were in the middle of a major life transition: moving out of our home (which we kept as a rental property), putting 75 percent of our belongings in storage, and temporarily moving in with my gracious mother-in-law while we searched for our next place to live. Our life was physically and emotionally in limbo, and my mind mirrored that chaos.

Even amid the busyness, I was trying to show up well for my kids. I knew they needed more from me—better schools, more structure, and a strong emotional foundation as they grew. But the weight of everything (work, transition, motherhood, expectations) left my mind tangled. I couldn't focus. I felt scattered, reactive, and mentally overstimulated. It was like my brain was trying to carry a dozen grocery bags with no cart in sight.

That season forced me to confront the cost of mental clutter. I realized I was constantly absorbing information and energy but never pausing long enough to process or reset. I was mentally clogged. After three months of uncertainty, we found our next house and moved yet again—this time out of storage and into our new home. The logistics were exhausting, but it was the mental clutter that nearly broke me. I was carrying too much (emotionally, logistically, physically) and it was showing up in my thoughts. I felt like I was living in fast-forward but mentally frozen at the same time.

That's when I began intentionally fighting for stillness. My walks became sacred—pockets of peace where I could breathe, think, and feel again. I left my phone behind and let nature and body movement do their healing work. I started gratitude journaling, deeply reflecting on the good things I still had, even in the mess. That practice grounded me. It reminded me that clarity comes from noticing what's already working. I also doubled down on affirmations. Not the fluffy kind, but intentional rewiring:

- *I am doing the best I can with what I have.*

- *I can handle hard things with grace.*

- *This season is preparing me for the next.*

These small but powerful shifts in my mental dialogue slowly helped clear the fog. I was no longer just reacting; I was beginning to respond with more clarity, more intention, and more presence.

Reclaiming My Mind

That tipping point forced me to stop and ask: *What am I doing?* And more importantly, *What am I allowing into my mental space that no longer serves me?* My walks became nonnegotiable. Even if they were short, they were mine. I listened to engaging music and let my brain untangle itself while my feet moved forward. I started gratitude journaling more intentionally. Not just writing down things I was grateful for, but processing the weight of what I was carrying and grounding myself in what was still good. And I leaned hard into affirmations. Not just feel-good statements, but real mental reframing:

- *This is temporary. I can do hard things.*

- *I'm allowed to hone my voice and set boundaries without guilt.*

- *Peace is a priority, not a luxury.*

These small habits helped me breathe again. They reminded me that I didn't have to keep absorbing more. I could choose what stayed in my mind. Clearing the clutter didn't happen overnight, but slowly, the fog lifted. I began to show up not just for my work or my business, but for myself.

Mind Matters

Your mind can be a beautiful meadow with flourishing flowers, or it can be cesspool of waste. What we think matters infinitely more than what we speak. Our thoughts and words are intrinsically connected. What we think becomes the real-life projector of our feelings and emotions, directly influencing the quality of our lives.

Since I was a little girl twirling in my mom's rose garden, I've been a dreamer. I'd visualize the things I wanted to accomplish. I dreamt of coming to America at a time when that seemed impossible. I dreamt of becoming an author and, one day, a *New York Times* bestselling author. Those dreams have grown over time. Now, I want my words to make an impact, to serve a greater purpose. How that will play out entirely is still unfolding, but the seed I planted long ago has already begun to sprout.

I once heard Judge Judy say something to this effect: If you didn't make it in your twenties, do it your thirties. If you didn't do in your thirties, do it in your forties, or your fifties or even your sixties. Nothing stands in our way more than the progress-blocking thoughts swirling in our minds.

Planting Seeds

The power of the mind is extraordinary. What you think, you create. What you focus on, you attract. The challenge lies in aligning your thoughts with the life you want to live. When I was pregnant with my first son, I wrote affirmations that reflected my dreams for him— everything from his appearance to his character. I even included something as specific as green eyes. No one in my family has had green eyes for generations, but when he was born, he had the most stunning pair of green eyes I'd ever seen. Whether it was divine intervention, the power of intention, or pure coincidence, I'll never know. What I do know is that my mind was focused and clear. I fed it positivity, intention, and purpose, and my reality reflected that.

The power of the spoken word is something I learned early. Speak what you want, then back it up with action. Our brains are wired to focus on what we repeatedly feed it. It's why affirmations work; they train your subconscious to filter out distractions and focus on opportunities that align with your goals. I remember a time when I fed my mind doubts, and it was like planting weeds in my garden. They grew faster than I could pull them. Once I consciously shifted my focus, the results were almost immediate.

Planting seeds is about daily action. Start small. If your goal is better health, your seed might be a ten-minute walk every morning. If you want to write a book, your seed could be writing five hundred words a day. If you're seeking mindfulness, your seed might be five minutes of gratitude journaling each night. Keep in mind that the habits you nurture today will bloom into the life you want tomorrow.

REFLECTIONS

Reclaim Your Mental Space

Activity	Action Step	Reflection Prompt
Music therapy	Create a playlist of songs that calm or uplift you.	The song that lifted my mood the most was _____ because _____.
Creative outlet	Draw, paint, bake, or try another creative activity.	I created _____. The process helped me feel _____.
Write	Journal for ten minutes about what's on your mind.	The thought I didn't realize I was holding onto was _____. Letting it out made me feel _____.
Digital Detox	Unplug from social media or devices for one hour.	During my detox, I spent my time _____. It made me feel _____.

A clear mind is a powerful mind. Take the first step today to reclaim your mental space because you're worth it.

1. *Find your quiet space*: Sit or lie down in a comfortable, quiet spot where you won't be disturbed for five to ten minutes.

2. *Relax and focus*: Breathe deeply: Inhale for four seconds, hold for four, exhale for four.

3. *Visualize your cluttered mind*: Picture your mind as a messy closet; floor littered with clothes, and shoes. Things are strewn everywhere and it's difficult to navigate through the dishevelment.

4. *Declutter*: Imagine yourself gently sorting through the clutter. The clothes or shoes represent your thoughts, worries, or tasks. Ask yourself: *Does this thought serve me?* If it doesn't, imagine clearing out your closet to make more space. For tasks or worries you need to address, visualize placing them in a neat container labeled "later" and then attach a timeframe to tackle it.

5. *Create a calm environment*: As you declutter your mental space, replace the chaos with calm. Picture your mind as a sanctuary, your own personal escape. Maybe it's a candlelit meditation room, a breezy mountaintop, or a sun-drenched beach where the waves kiss the shore in rhythm with your breath.

6. *Tune into your senses*: What does the air feel like? Is it warm and still, or cool and crisp? What colors wrap around you? Soft creams? Deep blues? Lush greens? Can you hear birds in the distance, the rustle of trees, or the soothing crash of waves? Is there a scent? Lavender, eucalyptus, maybe fresh rain on the earth? Don't just see it. Feel it. Breathe it in. Let this imagined space soothe you. Make it yours— somewhere you can return to whenever your mind begins to spiral.

7. *Set your positive intention*: Once the space feels clear and peaceful, imagine placing a positive word or phrase in the center of your mind-space. *Examples: Tranquility, Focus, Passion, I am Enough.* Imagine a soft glow of light illuminating that word and fill your mind with positivity.

8. *Return to your day gently*: Take a few deep breaths and slowly bring your awareness back to the present.

Reflect:

- How does your mind feel now?

- What can you do today to keep your mind-space clear and peaceful?

- What "clutter" did you release?

- How did your mental space transform?

- What positive word or phrase did you choose, and why?

TAKEAWAYS

● *Mental clarity is the foundation for success*: A cluttered mind inhibits growth, while a focused mind empowers action.

● *Small steps lead to big changes*: Consistent habits like journaling, gratitude, and decluttering can transform your mental and emotional well-being.

● *Your thoughts shape your reality*: By nurturing positive, intentional thoughts, you plant the seeds for the life you desire.

● *You are the architect of your mental garden*: It's time to weed out what no longer serves you and grow the life you were meant for.

Chapter Twelve

The Power of Now

Always say yes to the present moment. What could be more futile, more insane, than to create inner resistance to what already is? What could be more insane than to oppose life itself, which is now and always now? Surrender to what is. Say yes to life—and see how life suddenly starts working for you rather than against you.

—Eckhart Tolle

There is a lie that mothers are often sold: *Someday* is when your dreams will finally matter. *Someday* is when you'll reclaim yourself, pursue your passions, and live the life you've imagined. But someday is not a promise. It's an illusion. The kids will always need something. The house will always demand attention. The list will never be done. What if you stopped waiting for the perfect moment and started taking messy, imperfect steps today? What if you gave yourself permission to honor your dreams while still being the amazing mom you are?

The power of now lies in its urgency, its honesty. Life doesn't pause for us to catch up. This chapter is your call to action to stop postponing your potential and embrace the beauty of doing *something* (no matter how small) right now.

Actions Speak Louder Than Words

The saddest tragedy is hearing people repeatedly talk about dreams they never act upon. Dreaming is essential, but without action, dreams stagnate. Shift from words to action: Stop telling people what you're going to do. Start showing them with your actions. Document your progress for yourself, not for outside validation.

But there's a deeper truth here: Sustained action only comes from learning how to be present. Not racing ahead to the "what ifs," not ruminating on what's already passed, but meeting the moment you're in. Fully. Honestly. With open hands.

In 2022, my husband and I took on a massive challenge: transforming our long-term rental into an

Airbnb. It required gutting the house, navigating permits, designing the space, and furnishing it on a budget—all while managing other responsibilities. Needless to say, it was a long and arduous road. Some workdays were fourteen hours long. But the work never stopped. It was always top of mind. My nights were inundated with research and searching Facebook Marketplace for furniture, swings, and other items for the house. I handled the interior and garden design of the property and permits in addition to furnishing, while my husband oversaw construction and did a lot of the work himself. Every step was grueling but worth it. Three months later, we launched, and the pride we felt was indescribable.

The lesson? *Act more than you speak.* The harder you work on your dream, the greater the reward. Looking back, what kept me going was *presence.* I wasn't fixated on whether the property would be booked every night or whether every detail would be perfect. I had to surrender the outcome and root myself in *what I could do in that moment.* One choice. One task. One step.

That mindset—being fully in the moment—was a quiet superpower. When we're present, we're not drowning in future anxiety or paralyzed by past regrets. We're clear. We're grounded. We're able to listen to our inner wisdom instead of outside noise. We often resist the present moment because it demands something uncomfortable: acceptance. Of what's not perfect. Of what's hard. Of what's unfinished. But acceptance is not defeat—it's the starting point of real, empowered action. When you stop fighting the moment you're in, you reclaim the energy to move forward.

The lesson is to act more than you speak. But also: *Be more than you project.* The more rooted you are in the present, the more effective and meaningful your actions become. That's where clarity lives. That's where progress happens.

Creating a *Now* Mindset

American novelist Janet Dailey once wrote, "Someday is not a day of the week."[1] Waiting until the kids are grown, the house is quieter, or the stars align will only delay your progress. Instead, adopt a *now mindset.* Ask yourself: "What small action can I take today?" Break big goals into manageable steps. Celebrate small wins to build momentum.

The 5-Minute Rule

The 5-Minute Rule is a powerful way to overcome procrastination and inertia. The premise is simple: Commit to working on a task for just five minutes. Often, getting started is the hardest part, and once you begin, you'll likely keep going.

This method works because it reduces overwhelm. Big tasks feel less daunting when you break them into small, manageable chunks. It also builds momentum. Even small actions create a sense of accomplishment, fueling motivation to do more. Even more important, the 5-Minute Rule eliminates excuses. Everyone can spare five minutes, so it's harder to justify putting things off.

The Hidden Cost of Distractions

Distractions are everywhere—scrolling social media, binge-watching TV, or the endless loop of chores. While indulgences are okay, unchecked distractions can be a detriment to your dreams. The first step is recognizing what distracts you most and then creating boundaries. For instance, instead of folding laundry as the dryer buzzes, use that time to work on your goals. Laundry will always be there; your dreams might not. Establish routines where you limit distractions. Set a timer for focused work sessions and reward yourself after completing a task. You'll feel productive and still have time to unwind.

Multitasking might seem like a badge of honor, but it often dilutes your efforts. Focus on one goal at a time to ensure your energy isn't scattered. For example, if you're working on growing your online jewelry business, resist the temptation to start a new side hustle. Instead, pour your energy into mastering your craft, improving your marketing, and refining your processes. Success is built by doing the right things well.

The Center Stage Pyramid

The center stage pyramid is a tool designed to help you focus your energy on what matters most by creating a hierarchy of goals. Instead of spreading yourself too thin, it invites you to move with intention—spotlighting one goal at a time—so your time, energy, and resources flow where they'll make the greatest impact.

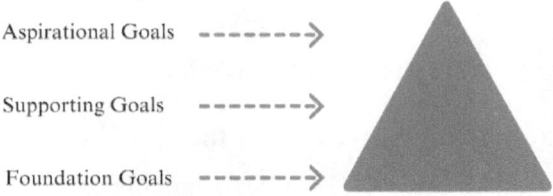

Aspirational Goals ------->

Supporting Goals ------->

Foundation Goals ------->

Base Level: The Foundation Goal

This is your main focus—the goal that will have the most transformative effect on your life right now. For example, if financial stability is a priority, you might build a savings habit or start a side hustle.

- *Action Step*: Identify one foundational goal and commit to it for a set period (three months, one year, etc.).

Middle Level: Supporting Goals

These are secondary goals that support or complement your foundation goal. For instance, if your foundation goal is building a side hustle, a supporting goal could be developing a time management routine to fit it into your schedule.

• *Action Step*: List two or three supporting goals and assign small, actionable tasks for each.

Top Level: Aspirational Goals

These are your long-term goals that you'll tackle once the foundation is secure. They're often big-picture visions, like writing a book or learning a new skill, that feel more attainable when your priorities are in order.

• *Action Step*: Keep a list of aspirational goals, revisiting them as your foundation and supporting goals progress.

Reevaluate your Center Stage Pyramid every three months to ensure it aligns with your current needs and aspirations. Combine the 5-Minute Rule with the Center Stage Pyramid by starting with your foundation goal. Those small, consistent actions will accumulate over time and lead to meaningful progress.

Let's say you're a mom with big dreams. Maybe you want to transition into a new career, show up more intentionally for your family, and feel strong in your body. Instead of chasing everything at once, the Center Stage Pyramid can help you organize your focus.

Foundation Goal

"Build a new skill to shift careers or start a business."

- *5-Minute Action*: Watch one short video, research a class, or write for five minutes.

Supporting Goal

"Create more presence and connection with my family, and prioritize my health to fuel my energy."

- *5-Minute Action*: Sit with your child and ask about their day. Do a five-minute stretch or movement session.

Aspirational Goal

"Cultivate a lifestyle where I feel purposeful, balanced, and fulfilled—financially, emotionally, and physically."

- *5-Minute Action*: Create a quiet space for mindfulness or journaling.

This approach honors your full identity as a woman, a mother, and an individual with purpose. You're not choosing one goal over another; you're stacking them in a way that makes progress possible without the burnout.

REFLECTIONS

What is one goal you've been putting off, and why? How can you take one small step toward it today?

_____

_____

Think about a moment you took action despite feeling unprepared. How did that turn out?

_____

_____

How would your life improve if you devoted just five minutes a day to something that ignites your fire?

_____

_____

What distractions are keeping you from your "now," and how can you minimize them?

_____

_____

How can your actions today set an example for your children about prioritizing dreams and goals?

_____

_____

THE POWER OF NOW

1. *Create your Center Stage Pyramid*

- Identify a foundational goal (your core focus).

- Define supporting goals that align with your foundation.

- Dream big by outlining your aspirational goal.

2. *Apply the 5-Minute Rule*

- Choose a goal from your Center Stage Pyramid.

● Spend just five minutes working toward it today—whether it's organizing your workspace, researching a class, or writing an outline for a project.

3. *Establish Nonnegotiable "Now Moments"*

● Dedicate at least fifteen minutes daily to yourself. Use this time for growth, mindfulness, or passion projects.

● Communicate this boundary to your family so they understand its importance.

4. *Set Visual Reminders*

● Place notes or vision board images in high-traffic areas of your home to remind you of your goals and why they matter.

5. *Track Your Progress*

● Use a journal or app to log small wins and reflect on how taking action daily is moving you closer to your aspirations.

TAKEAWAYS

- *The best time is now*: Life's demands will never slow down. Taking action today (no matter how small) is the key to building momentum.

- *Clarity over chaos*: The Center Stage Pyramid helps you filter what matters most and ensures your energy is aligned with your aspirations.

- *Small steps matter*: The 5-Minute Rule eliminates procrastination. Starting small is still starting, and it builds confidence and consistency.

- *Messy is okay*: Perfect conditions don't exist. Embrace the messiness of beginnings, knowing that progress is always better than perfection.

- *Action over words*: Dreams only grow when you nurture them with action. Start showing yourself and others what you're capable of doing.

Chapter Thirteen

Emotional Scrolling

I hope you will go out and let stories ... life ... happen to you, and that you will work with these stories. Water them with your blood and tears and your laughter till they bloom, till you yourself burst into bloom.
—Clarissa Pinkola Estés

You pick up your phone for a moment of escape. *Just five minutes*, you tell yourself. But somehow, an hour slips by and you've gone from laughing at baby goats to envying someone's flawless kitchen, perfect abs, or family vacation in Santorini. You close the app feeling drained, inadequate, and strangely, lonelier than before.

Welcome to emotional scrolling. It doesn't just steal your time; it hijacks your confidence, your joy, and your presence. It feeds you highlight reels while your real life—messy, beautiful, and full of meaning—fades into the background.

The Cost of Scrolling

Social media dangles the illusion of connection, but often leaves us feeling isolated and lonely. It's like standing outside a beautifully lit window, peering into someone else's seemingly perfect world, wondering, *Why doesn't my life sparkle like that?* The truth? Those shimmering lives are often illusions—built on filters, edits, and curated moments that mask the messiness of reality. Intellectually, we know this, but emotionally it's hard to look away. Every second spent scrolling is a quiet thief, stealing time from what truly matters—our dreams, our loved ones, and the fleeting beauty of the present moment.

The Psychology Behind Scrolling

Social media platforms are designed to keep us hooked, and the science behind it lies in how our brains respond to dopamine—a chemical messenger associated with pleasure and reward. Every like, follow, notification, view, or comment triggers a small dopamine hit, reinforcing the behavior of checking our phones constantly. For moms especially, this hit of validation can feel like a rare treat amidst a day filled with endless responsibilities. Over time, this creates a cycle of dependency where we crave rewards and feel a sense of loss or emptiness when they're absent.

This constant craving for social validation mirrors other addictive behaviors, like overeating, gambling, or alcohol addiction, where intermittent rewards keep us engaged. The uncertainty of what we'll see next (a funny video, an uplifting post, or a shocking headline) only heightens the addictive nature of scrolling. It's the digital equivalent of pulling the lever on a slot machine, hoping for a big win.

How can you break free from this life-draining habit? Recognize the pattern and consciously interrupt it. Apps that track screen time or block social media after a certain limit can be helpful tools. Replace scrolling with healthier dopamine sources, like exercise, spending time outdoors, or engaging in creative pursuits.

The Instant-Gratification Trap

We moms are wired for efficiency—getting things done quickly and juggling multiple priorities. Social media feeds into this by offering instant gratification. With a few clicks, we're entertained, connected, or validated. While this feels good in the moment, it rewires our brains to prioritize quick rewards over long-term satisfaction. This mindset spills over into other areas of life, making us impatient with processes that take time—whether it's pushing a career goal, building relationships, or working on personal growth. Social media's advancement and immediacy conditions us to expect everything in life to come just as quickly, and when it doesn't, we often feel frustration or discouragement.

Practice delayed gratification by setting small, meaningful goals that require effort and time. Celebrate incremental progress instead of seeking immediate result. Develop habits like journaling or meditation to strengthen your focus and patience. When tempted to scroll, ask yourself: *Will this help me get closer to what I really want, or is it just a distraction?*

Cyber Comparison

How many times have you looked at another mom's Instagram feed and thought, *Why doesn't my life look like that?* I know I have. There was a time when scrolling felt like my lifeline—a way to escape the chaos of life for a few minutes. When my kids were much younger, I'd pick up my phone while they were napping or in between working on a project, telling myself, *Just a quick break.* I'd start with innocent intentions—catching up on a friend's post or looking for a new dinner recipe. Before I knew it, I'd stumbled into a rabbit hole of picture-perfect family vacations, flawless outfits, and immaculate kitchens that seemed light-years away from my reality.

One day, I found myself staring at a fitness influencer's post. She had just had her baby a few months earlier and looked incredible—abs and all. Meanwhile, I was sitting there with my hair in a top knot wearing raggedy sweatpants, toys strewn about, and a mountain of unfiled paper-work, feeling like I'd failed. I started comparing everything: her body, her clean house, her seemingly endless energy. My mind spiraled, questioning why I couldn't keep up.

But here's the catch: I wasn't seeing her reality. I wasn't seeing her messy moments, her struggles, or the team of people likely creating the picture-perfect set of her home. I was comparing my behind-the-scenes dishevelment to her carefully curated highlight reel. That realization didn't come right away though. It took a lot of intentional reflection and pulling myself out of the scrolling habit to understand the toll it had taken on me emotionally—and the time it had stolen from my family.

Online Validation

Have you found yourself scrolling through social media and feeling the gnawing sense of inadequacy? Maybe it's not even about the perfect images; it's the constant stream of *other people's accomplishments* that make you question your own. It could be a friend celebrating a promotion, a neighbor showing off her perfectly decorated home, or someone hitting fitness goals while you're trying to remember the last time you worked out.

These moments can chip away at your self-worth. Without realizing it, you start measuring your value against snapshots of someone else's life. Social media amplifies this tendency, turning the validation we seek from others into a subtle but relentless craving. Likes and comments become a form of approval, leaving us feeling invisible when they don't come.

But here's the truth: Your worth does not depend on someone else's approval. It doesn't live in a "like," or a "comment," or a "follower count." And when we outsource our validation to social media, we lose sight of the beauty of our real lives—the laughter of our kids, the strength we embody, and the quiet victories we achieve every day.

Reclaim Your Self-Worth

1. *Audit Your Online Environment*: Take a look at your social media feeds. Who are you following? If their content consistently leaves you feeling "less than," it's time to unfollow or mute them. Curate your feed to include inspiring, real, and positive influences that inspire without creating comparison.

2. *Set Boundaries with Social Media*: Create clear time limits for scrolling. Use tools or apps to set daily usage caps. When you limit exposure, you give yourself more mental and emotional space to focus on what profoundly matters.

3. *Shift Your Focus*: Start a gratitude practice that highlights *your* wins. At the end of each day, jot down three things you do well or are proud of, no matter how small. Over time, you'll train yourself to see your own worth without the need for external validation.

4. *Reinforce Affirmations*: Replace self-doubt with positive affirmations. Say them out loud or write them down: "My worth isn't defined by what others think." "I celebrate my own journey, no matter how different it looks."

5. *Model Healthy Behavior for Your Kids*: Remember, you children watch everything you do. Show them how to prioritize self-worth by speaking kindly about yourself and others, avoiding self-critical language, and emphasizing effort and growth over comparison.

REFLECTIONS

Prompt	Your Response
What specific times will you set for social media use?	
What activity will you replace scrolling with?	
Write an affirmation to remind yourself of your worth.	
Name three personal wins or moments of gratitude from today.	1. _____ 2. _____ 3. _____
What's one thing you admire about your life?	

TAKEAWAYS

• *Understand the cost of scrolling*: Every moment spent mindlessly scrolling is a moment taken from meaningful moments—time with your loved ones, pursuing your goals, or enjoying life offline. Recognize that scrolling is not a harmless habit; it impacts your emotional well-being and productivity.

• *Acknowledge the emotional toll of comparison*: Social media can negatively affect your self-worth and mental health by fostering feelings of inadequacy or comparison. It's crucial to understand that those perfect lives you see online are often curated illusions.

• *Break the dopamine cycle*: Scrolling provides quick dopamine hits, creating a cycle of desiring instant gratification. Breaking this cycle requires replacing it with healthier habits that offer long-term satisfaction, like hobbies, exercise, or connecting with loved ones.

• *Set boundaries for social media*: Create specific time limits for your screen time, such as no phones at the dinner table or leave your device in another room during family time. These small shifts can help reclaim your time and mental clarity.

- *Model healthy behavior for your kids*: Children duplicate what they see. By practicing mindful phone use, you teach your kids the value of presence, focus, and real-life connection.

- *Replace scrolling with intentional moments*: Use the time you'd spend scrolling for small but impactful actions: write down your goals, read a chapter of a book, take a walk, or simply enjoy a quiet moment.

Chapter Fourteen

Good MO

For any movement to gain momentum, one must start with a small action.

—Adam Braun

A single snowflake starts at the top of a hill. With one tiny push, it begins to roll, collecting more snow as it moves, growing larger and faster. By the time it reaches the bottom, it's an unstoppable force. That's momentum. Now imagine applying the same concept to your life, your goals, and your dreams. Building momentum is the secret ingredient to creating the life you desire.

Good MO (short for "good momentum") is about sustaining the force that keeps you moving forward. The repetitive actions, day in and day out, are what transform small steps into massive achievements. Momentum is what turns intentions into results. It's not glamorous, and it's often not fun. But it is effective. One of my closest friends, Sharia Bacchus, is the embodiment of momentum. From the outside, she might seem like a quiet, unassuming woman—someone you might not immediately peg as a trailblazer. But trust me when I say that she is a force of nature.

Sharia, a stay-at-home mom of four, made a bold decision most would never dare to make. She uprooted her family from the comforts of life in the United States and returned to her home country of Guyana, a place brimming with opportunity but also significant challenges. Most people would have felt daunted by the obstacles of moving to a developing country and starting over. Not Sharia. With sheer determination, unshakable discipline, and an unrelenting work ethic, she built a real estate business from scratch that turned into a thriving, respected empire. Her company quickly became the go-to real estate connection for international oil companies, governments, and corporations setting up shop in Guyana, a nation at the heart of the booming oil industry.

Sharia commanded success. She's now respected across the entire country, from local communities to the highest levels of government. Her name carries weight, her reputation speaks volumes, and her influence has created opportunities not just for her family, but for countless others who rely on her expertise and vision.

When I spent time with her a while back, I was completely in awe. Here is a woman who transformed her life through sheer grit and grace, pushing past every limitation. She is a powerhouse, a leader, and a role model for what can happen when you combine discipline with faith and a relentless drive to succeed. Her story is proof that momentum isn't about luck or talent; it's about consistently showing up, doing the work, and never losing sight of your goals. She built her success brick by brick, day by day, creating a legacy that will stand for generations.

If we want good MO in our lives, we must take action every single day. Think of it like running a marketing campaign. Every ad has a clear call to action (CTA). Without it, the customer is lost, unsure of the next step. Similarly, without a clear direction and purpose in our own lives, we waste energy spinning our wheels.

So what's your CTA? Maybe it's waking up earlier to journal or go to the gym. Maybe it's prioritizing family dinners. Whatever it is, it starts with caring enough to act. Excuses don't build momentum—consistency does.

Breaks: The Double-Edged Sword

Taking breaks can either recharge you or completely derail your progress. There's no middle ground here. A break can be either fuel or failure. If you're trying to build momentum, a break isn't a vacation; it's a strategic move. But most of the time it's used as an excuse.

I know how easy it is to get comfortable thinking, *I'll just take one day off and get back to it tomorrow.* That's a slippery slope. One day becomes two. Two becomes a week. Before you know it, you've fallen off track. And what happens then? You waste valuable time you can never get back.

When I committed to writing this book, I didn't allow myself the luxury of a weekend binge-watching shows or scrolling through my phone for hours. I was in the middle of something bigger. Every day I showed up, even when it was uncomfortable. Even when I didn't feel like it. The lesson? Breaks should refresh you, not sabotage you. They are not a free pass to stop moving; they are a chance to reset, refuel, and get back in the game.

The Art of Accountability

Momentum doesn't care about excuses; it thrives on accountability. If you can't hold yourself accountable, you're dead in the water. What's the cost of inaction? What do you risk losing when you don't show up? The answers to those questions should haunt you because they're real. This isn't just some feel-good rhetoric; it's survival. When you let things slide, the momentum you've built starts to erode. The longer you put things off, the harder it is to get back in the game. That's why accountability isn't negotiable. It really is your lifeline.

Take my Airbnb business. I didn't simply post the listing and hope for the best. I had to show up, even when I was exhausted or frustrated. I was the one cleaning, the one fixing everything from broken garbage disposals to repainting doors. I wasn't waiting for someone else to do it. If it needed to be done, I did it. And let me be real— there were nights when I was ready to throw in the towel. I'd be driving on the turnpike at ten p.m., tears in my eyes, wondering why I was doing it all. In those moments I felt like quitting. But I didn't. Every task I completed, no matter how small, brought me closer to success. I didn't just want a profitable business. I wanted a powerhouse.

My solid sense of accountability to myself and to my guests was the key to making that happen. In building my business, I often put myself in my clients' footsteps, trying to understand what they might value or appreciate. And it's with that mindset I hold myself to a high level of excellence. Now, every time I think about slacking off, I remember how it felt to achieve that success. I remember that every detail mattered. Accountability is the fuel that turns your efforts into results.

Overcoming Inertia

Have you ever sat staring at a long to-do list, completely overwhelmed by where to begin? Or worse, procrastinated so long that starting felt like scaling a mountain? That's inertia at work—the invisible force that keeps you stuck in place. It's like trying to push a car from a dead stop. The hardest part is getting it to budge even an inch. But once it starts rolling, momentum takes over and the effort becomes effortless.

Inertia is the resistance to change. It's the mental weight and fatigue that makes the first step feel impossible. The good news? You don't need to conquer everything at once to overcome it. You just need to *start*. One small action (a five-minute task, a single phone call, or even writing one sentence) can break the cycle of inaction and ignite the power of momentum.

Tips for Overcoming inertia:

1. *Set a timer*: Commit to five minutes. Often starting with a short burst of focused energy leads to much more.

2. *Break It Down*: Instead of attempting to tackle a giant task, pick one small, manageable piece. For example, if you're overwhelmed by creating social media content for your business, start with just one video or one post.

3. *Celebrate Progress*: Don't wait for the "perfect time" or for everything to be in place. Start messy if you must. Momentum doesn't care about flawlessness.

Inertia thrives on indecision and fear. The ultimate trick is to trick it back: Act before you can talk yourself out of it. That tiny first step is all you need to shift from being stuck to being unstoppable!

Discipline in Momentum

Motivation is a fickle friend. It shows up when you're inspired but disappears when the going gets tough. Discipline, on the other hand, is the reliable partner you need for the long haul. If motivation lights the spark, discipline keeps the fire burning. Momentum isn't built on the days when you *feel* like showing up; it's built on the days when you don't. Discipline bridges the gap between where you are and where you want to be. It's what transforms fleeting inspiration into lasting progress.

How to Cultivate Discipline:

Create a routine. Habits thrive on consistency. Set specific times for key actions, like making the bed every morning or going for a walk before dinner. Make the actions nonnegotiable. Identify one or two actions that you'll do no matter what—whether it's writing one hundred words a day or working out for fifteen minutes. Don't just reward the result; reward the effort too. Showing up consistently is an achievement in itself.

Think of discipline as an investment in your future self. Every minuscule action, done repeatedly, compounds over time. It might not feel exciting in the moment, but it builds a foundation of momentum that will carry you through any challenge. Discipline is the secret of every successful person. It's how you go from wishing for progress to creating it, one deliberate action at a time.

REFLECTIONS

Momentum-Building Table

Focus Area	Prompt	Plan of Action
Start small.	What is one small action you can take today to move closer to your goal?	
Clarify your why.	Why does this goal matter to you? How will it impact your life and others?	
Build discipline.	What daily habit can you commit to, even when motivation fades?	
Identify resistance.	What fears, excuses, or obstacles have kept you from starting? How can you overcome them?	

Focus Area	Prompt	Plan of Action
Take accountability.	Who can you share your goal with to help keep you accountable?	
Reframe setbacks.	How will you view and learn from setbacks to maintain momentum instead of giving up?	
Define your long-term vision.	What does success look like six months or a year from now? What can you do today to align with your vision?	

TAKEAWAYS

- *Momentum starts small*: You don't have to undertake a radical transformation overnight. Start with one small action to create the spark of momentum.

- *Discipline fuels momentum*: Motivation may waver, but discipline ensures you show up and keep the progress going, even when it's hard.

- *Inertia is the enemy*: Overcome resistance to start by focusing on manageable tasks. Action—even imperfect action—breaks the cycle of inaction.

- *Consistency builds the habit*: Momentum thrives on routine. When you prioritize regular, repeatable actions, they become second nature.

- *Accountability matters*: Share your goals and progress with someone you trust. Support and encouragement can keep you moving forward.

- *Every effort counts*: Remember, it's not about perfection but progress. Every small win adds up to significant results over time.

- *Your momentum is your power*: The more you move, the more you grow. Whether it's personal development, health goals, or career ambitions, momentum is the force that turns dreams into reality.

Part Two

Taking Center Stage: Owning the Spotlight

Chapter Fifteen

The Window of Self-Discovery

The more you know, the more you realize you don't know.
—Aristotle

What if the greatest discoveries about yourself are waiting behind a window you've never opened? A window that reveals hidden strengths, unseen blind spots, and untapped potential. This window isn't made of glass; it's built from self-awareness and growth. Let's crack it open together.

The Johari Window: A Lens for Self-Discovery

The Johari Window is a remarkable tool for reflection and awareness. This concept, developed in 1955 by psychologist Joseph Luft and Harry Ingram, provides a framework that reveals the layers of self-awareness: known and unknown to ourselves and to others.[1]

Johari Window

Known to Self	Not Known to Self
Open Self (known to self and others)	**Blind Self** (not known to self but known to others)
Hidden Self (known to self but not others)	**Unknown Self** (not known to self or others)

Breaking Down the Window

Open Self

This is the version of you that's transparent—what you and others both know. It could be your talent as a hairstylist, your love for fitness, or your knack for organizing events. I used to keep my entrepreneurial goals to myself, worried that people might think I was being overly ambitious or setting myself up for failure. But the moment I started sharing my aspirations, I realized that people wanted to help me. When I told a close Realtor friend about my idea for managing short-term rentals and finding real estate opportunities, she connected me with many resources and went above and beyond to support me.

Blind Self

This refers to the things about you that others notice but you are unaware of. Maybe you're the first to panic in a crisis, or perhaps you inspire others without realizing it. These are our blind spots. At a meeting, my team did an exercise where we wrote down one positive truth about each person in the room. By the end of the evening, I held a paper filled with attributes others saw in me—qualities I didn't know I had. It was a wake-up call. Here I was, moving through life without seeing the true value I brought to others, only to have it pointed out to me.

Hidden Self

These are the secrets and aspirations you keep to yourself. Maybe you dream of starting a business, but fear holds you back. Or perhaps you have a talent that only your shower walls have heard about. For years, I kept my desire to write a book to myself. But deep down, I knew it was more than a mere desire. It was my calling. I remember the first time I mentioned it to my mom, and in response she confidently said, "Go for it! You can do it!" That simple encouragement and her continued check-ins on my progress became fuel for my dream. The moment I stopped hiding that part of me, opportunities and inspiration started flowing in ways I had never imagined.

Unknown Self

This is the most intriguing quadrant. It represents untapped potential. Adversity often unlocks this space, revealing strengths you never imagined you possessed. When my father passed away, my mom faced unimaginable challenges as a young widow. She could have crumbled. The grief and hardship she experienced raising children in a third world country with little resources was like attempting to wade through quicksand. It seemed impossible. Instead, these unfortunate events unleashed her potential as the strongest person I know. Her journey through adversity revealed an unstoppable fight that was always within her but had never been tested. I had the honor of seeing her rise into the Khaleesi she is today. And the best part? I have benefitted from her example. Through her, I found my grit. My passion. My moxie. It was within me all along.

Embrace the Uncomfortable

Growth never comes from comfort zones. Imagine walking in wet shoes—unpleasant, right? But sometimes discomfort, whether physical or mental, is the catalyst for change. Consider the habits that are holding you back. Maybe it's staying up too late, procrastinating, or avoiding difficult conversations. Change isn't about waiting until you "feel ready." It's about creating an internal push to act even when it's inconvenient.

Marie Forleo says it best: "Everything is figureoutable."[2] You can figure out how to break habits, build momentum, and move closer to your goals, but only if you're willing to embrace discomfort as part of the process.

Blind Spots

Just like cars, we all have blind spots—areas we can't see without help. These blind spots can hinder progress if we don't take steps to uncover them. This is where feedback becomes essential. Seek out trusted people (a coach, mentor, or friend) who can offer honest insight.

Be selective. Choose advisors who have achieved what you aspire to. If you want relationship advice, talk to someone in a healthy, thriving partnership. If you're launching a business, consult someone who has succeeded in your industry. A thoughtful, experienced perspective can help you spot the areas you're missing and provide actionable guidance.

Comfort vs. Growth Table

For a long time, I used to shy away from difficult feedback. I saw it as criticism—something to defend myself against rather than grow from. But I've learned that feedback, when received with openness, is a powerful tool for transformation. Growth rarely comes without discomfort. In fact, some of the most meaningful changes in my life have started with a willingness to let go of old habits and step into new, sometimes uncomfortable territory.

This table reflects that shift: small but intentional moves from comfort to growth, and the potential outcomes when you choose to lean into discomfort instead of avoiding it.

Comfort to Let Go	Discomfort to Embrace	Anticipated Results
Late-night snacking	Eat dinner by 7:00 or 7:30 p.m. each night, and then be done with food for the day.	Get better sleep and improve your overall health.
Avoiding difficult feedback	Ask for constructive input.	Aim for personal growth with clearer blind spots.
Scrolling social media at night	Read or journal before bed.	Have better focus and a calmer mind.

The difference between staying stuck and growing lies in what you're willing to let go of and what you're brave enough to embrace.

Explore the Johari Window

The Emotional Lens

Use the Johari Window to assess your emotional blind spots. Are there feelings you avoid or suppress? For instance, if anger makes you uncomfortable, how might that affect your relationships? For years, I thought of myself as a master of pleasing people and keeping my cool. I avoided expressing anger and the things that upset me, believing it made me a better person. I realized that my avoidance of anger (or uncomfortable conversations) and addressing situations wasn't helpful. It was sending the wrong message. While I'm not one to shout and scream, I have every right and reason to share my displeasure if it affects the foundational principles I have established for my life. Not addressing things disrupts the future and leads to poor outcomes. Remember, people pleasers do one thing: They please others, leaving themselves and their feelings out of the equation.

Relationships as Mirrors

Your relationships can reflect what's hidden or unknown within yourself. When conflicts or misunderstandings arise, it's worth asking: *What's my role in this? Is this showing me a blind spot or something I've been hiding?* A friend once pointed out that I rarely share my struggles, even though I encourage others to open up. It's true, *I am* someone who rarely focuses on the hardships. I tend to be optimistic even through difficulties. It's my superpower and my kryptonite. The truth? I am neither made of steel nor am I infallible. I discovered that having vulnerabilities is okay. I started sharing small things—a difficult workday or a parenting challenge. To my surprise, these moments deepened my friendships and made me feel more connected.

Cultural Perspective

Cultural norms and societal expectations can heavily influence what we keep in our "hidden" or "unknown" selves. Sometimes these pressures can limit us. As women, especially within our culture, there's an unspoken expectation to endure, to push through pain, and to get things done—no matter the cost. For me, there was never an excuse not to handle what needed handling. Whether it was heavy lifting or working tirelessly, I've always risen to the challenge.

But that relentless "just get it done" mentality came with consequences. During the setup of my Airbnb, I carried anything and everything, determined to do it all. I've always prided myself on being strong and capable, but what I didn't realize was the toll it was taking on my body. Over time, that heavy lifting materialized in my body as extreme stress and then became something more: cystocele.

It's not a comfortable topic to bring up, but it's exactly the kind of thing we need to speak about. The silent pain many of us carry—physical, emotional, and mental—often goes unnoticed because we're conditioned to stay quiet. We dismiss it as part of the load we must bear.

But this shouldn't be our reality. We need to stop dismissing our pain as just part of the burden we must bear. It's time to talk about it, to acknowledge it, and to prioritize our health. Talking about the tolls we endure gives a voice to what so many others are experiencing and serves as a reminder that it's okay to ask for help, to set boundaries, and to put our health first.

Setting Intentions

Each quadrant of the Johari Window offers an opportunity to grow, but it requires deliberate effort. By setting weekly or monthly intentions, you can actively work to expand your "open self" or uncover hidden potential. I once set a goal to address my "hidden self" by being more forthcoming about my goals. I'd always downplayed my ambition to write a book, worried people would think it was unrealistic. On one of my visits to Guyana, I mentioned to my good friend's sister that I was finally doing it, expecting her to just nod in acknowledgement or simply say, "That's good." Instead, she enthusiastically congratulated me and asked how she could help. She quite literally started thinking of all the people who could be good connections in my writing and publishing process. She even messaged me recently, asking how my writing was going and to put her down for a pre-order. That one conversation provided a burst of encouragement I didn't even know I needed.

REFLECTIONS

1. *Map your own Johari Window*: Create a simple table with the four quadrants: Open Self, Hidden Self, Blind Spots, and Unknown Self. Write down what you know or suspect belongs in each area. Ask a trusted friend, mentor, or partner for feedback on your blind spots to gain new insights.

2. *Share something hidden*: Choose one thing from your hidden-self quadrant (an interest, talent, or thought) and share it with someone you trust. Notice how it feels to let others in.

3. *Seek feedback*: Identify one area where you'd like to grow (public speaking, leadership, relationships) and ask for constructive feedback from someone who excels in that area.

4. *Reflect on the unknown*: Journal about experiences where you surprised yourself—times you handled adversity, discovered a hidden skill, or overcame fear. What untapped potential could be waiting for you?

5. *Set an intention*: Pick one actionable goal to expand your "Open Self" or explore your "Unknown Self" (taking a class, tackling a fear, or seeking mentorship).

6. *Embrace discomfort*: Identify a habit, routine, or fear that feels like a safety net but might be holding you back. Take one small step to face or let go of it this week.

TAKEAWAYS

- *Self-awareness is power*: Self-awareness is about using your knowledge to unlock growth. The Johari Window is a tool for that very transformation.

- *Feedback fuels growth*: Constructive feedback is a mirror that shows us what we can't see ourselves. Be open to listening and learning.

- *Hidden gems await*: The hidden-self quadrant often holds untapped potential—skills, ideas, or feeling waiting to be expressed. Sharing them can strengthen relationships and open doors.

- *The unknown is an opportunity*: Life's challenges often reveal capabilities we never knew we had. See your unknown self (your potential) as an invitation to grow.

- *Discomfort leads to discovery*: The path to personal growth is rarely easy. By stepping out of your comfort zone, you create momentum and unlock new possibilities.

- *We are all works in progress*: No matter your age, stage, or achievements, there's always room to learn, grow, and evolve. Stay curious, and keep exploring.

The Struggle Breakthrough

When it is dark enough, you can see the stars.
—Ralph Waldo Emerson

We live in a world that glorifies ease. Convenience is king, and struggle? It's the enemy. Society trains us to avoid it, sidestep it, and, if possible, outsource it. But struggle has its benefits. See it as the toll you pay for anything worthwhile. If you want to break through, you have to be willing to break down some walls first.

Struggle isn't glamorous. It doesn't make a cute Instagram story. It's ugly, messy, exhausting. It tests your patience, your confidence, your will to keep going.

Without it, transformation doesn't happen. Yet the ugly moments are the ones that shape you the most.

But transformation happens. I learned this the hard way when I was 7,000 words into writing this book. I hit a wall. A big, suffocating, "I have nothing left to say" kind of wall. The words stopped flowing. I felt like I had wrung out every ounce of creativity and inspiration. I tried to push through, but it felt forced, uninspired. So I paused. That hiatus (though frustrating) was exactly what I needed. It gave me space to breathe, to reconnect with my purpose. When I returned, I had clarity, and the words poured out like they had been waiting for me all along.

That struggle was my *breakthrough*. It's found in the moments of doubt, exhaustion, and frustration that shape you. You don't get to skip the hard parts. The hard parts are the whole dang point.

Pushing Through the "Meh" Moments

Starting something new? That's easy. The beginning is intoxicating. But keeping that energy alive? The midway point is where people quit. The monotony sets in. The excitement fades. You hit the dreaded "meh" phase where everything feels flat, uninspired, and you start questioning why you even started in the first place. It's in these moments, the *meh* moments, where you must decide: *Am I going to quit and blend in with the masses, or am I going to push through and come out on top?*

But here's the kicker: The difference between success and mediocrity is what you do in those meh moments.

- Do you show up anyway?

- Do you do the work when no one's clapping?

- Do you push through even when your motivation is MIA?

If you only put in the effort when you *feel* like it, you'll never get anywhere. Your breakthrough comes from the discipline of showing up even when you'd rather binge Netflix or scroll your phone.

Stuff Most People Won't Do

How do you determine your edge? It's typically found in doing the things that the masses refuse to do. That's your superpower. Most people will dabble, quit, and make excuses. You? You do what they won't. Success doesn't last on a burst of motivation; it thrives on consistency, on doing the work when no one is watching, when no one is cheering.

I don't care what industry you're in. Success belongs to the people who are willing to grind when others are slacking off. Want to be a better entrepreneur? A better mom? A stronger leader? Do the work that's inconvenient, uncomfortable, and unglamorous.

If you're a childcare provider, get CPR-certified, learn child psychology, *become the best.* If you're an artist, study color theory, master composition, explore new mediums. If you're in business, know your numbers, refine your pitch, outlearn everyone in the room.

Take my eldest son. He started playing piano in the third grade. For a while, his interest waned, and he struggled to stay consistent. When he wasn't practicing or taking it seriously, I had to pause his lessons. I told him I wasn't going to spend money for classes if he wasn't going to put in the time and effort. Over time, though, he found his rhythm again—literally and figuratively. Through daily practice and stick-to-itiveness, his skill has blossomed, and now, watching him play feels like witnessing art in motion.

But that beauty was born from struggle: his frustration with hitting the wrong notes, his desire to quit, and the discipline I nudged him toward, even when it was uncomfortable for both of us. Stop switching your dreams like you switch your outfits. Commitment is rare. Consistency is even rarer. Do one thing, do it damn well, and become so good you can't be ignored.

The Struggle Breakthrough Table

The Struggle You Are Facing	The Excuse	The Solution
"I don't have time."	"I'm too busy."	Cut distractions. Make it a priority.
"I'm not good enough."	"I don't have talent."	Skill > talent. Put in the reps.
"I don't know how."	"I'm not tech-savvy."	Google it. Take a class. You can figure it out.
"I feel stuck."	"I've hit a wall."	Step away. Reconnect with your why, then return.
"No one supports me."	"I feel alone."	Find mentors. Seek community, but don't wait for permission.

REFLECTIONS

Breakthroughs and Competitive Edge

1. The struggle I keep avoiding but need to face is:

_____.

2. If I push through this struggle, I will gain:

_____.

3. One small action I can take today to lean in to discomfort is:

_____.

4. The last time I struggled and came out stronger, I learned that I am:

_____.

5. A skill I need to sharpen to gain a competitive edge is:

_____.

6. If I commit to mastering this skill for the next 90 days, I will be able to:

_____.

7. The excuse I tell myself the most is:

_____.

8. If I refuse to let that excuse control me, my next move will be:

_____.

9. One thing I admire in successful people that I need to start implementing is:

_____.

10. By the end of this year, I want to look back and say:

_____.

TAKEAWAYS

- *Struggle isn't optional.* If it's hard, you're on the right path.

- *Commit to the "meh" moments.* Discipline > motivation. Show up anyway.

- *Identify your competitive edge, your superpower.* What are you willing to do that most people aren't?

- *Eliminate excuses.* If something matters, you'll find a way. If not, you'll find an excuse.

- *Find small ways to level up daily.* One skill. One habit. One uncomfortable action—every single day.

- *The shortcut is always the long way disguised as something easier.* Take the long way. Do the work. Earn your breakthrough.

- *Every step toward your breakthrough counts.* The grind is the gateway to growth. The pain you push through today is the strength you carry tomorrow.

Chapter Seventeen

Quiet the Voices of the Naysayers

You have two choices. You can keep running and hiding and blaming the world for your problems, or you can stand up for yourself and decide to be somebody important.
—*Sidney Sheldon*

Who or what contributes to all the noise in your life? The noise isn't always loud, but it is persistent. It seeps in through doubt, unsolicited opinions, and the subtle (or not-so-subtle) discouragement of others. Sometimes it comes from those closest to you who, whether intentionally or not, diminish your ambitions with their skepticism.

Broadcasting your goals can be liberating. But sometimes it's like handing someone a match while standing in a room full of gasoline. Not everyone will celebrate your vision. Some will doubt your ability to achieve it. Others may actively root against you out of jealousy, fear, or their own unresolved insecurities.

Imagine excitedly telling someone you're writing a book, and they respond, "That's nice, but do you really think people will read it?" Those words, seemingly harmless, can plant doubt. Throughout life, you will encounter people who will scoff at your dreams. The question is, will you let them dictate your future? Or will you guard your vision the way you guard your heart, protecting it from those who can't see what you see?

Think of the people in your life as weights: Some anchor you, keeping you grounded and secure. Others are burdens, dragging you down with negativity, doubt, and energy-draining conversations. If you're always defending your ambitions to someone, it's time to consider their place in your journey.

Not everyone deserves front-row seats to your life. Some people should watch from the nosebleed section— or better yet, outside the stadium entirely. This isn't about arrogance; it's about self-preservation. If you are constantly explaining yourself, justifying your dreams, or shrinking to make others comfortable, then you aren't truly living life on your terms.

NPCs

My kids recently taught me about the term NPC—a non-player character in a video game. NPCs exist in the game world, but they don't make their own choices. They follow pre-programmed scripts, repeating the same lines, standing in the same place, never evolving. Do you know people like that? People who settle, who don't question, who don't aspire? People who say things like, "That's just the way things are," or "I'd love to do that, but . . ." and never take action?

The NPC mindset, when applied to real life, is a metaphor for living on autopilot—functioning, but not fully engaged. It's a way of moving through the world by reacting rather than creating, conforming rather than choosing. And while it might feel safe or familiar, it can quietly and powerfully hinder our growth in profound ways. Living like an NPC also keeps us disconnected from our emotions, from our intuition, and from each other. We go through the motions. We scroll. We work. We parent. We perform. But we don't feel deeply or act from our passions. Over time, this dulls our aliveness. We might function well enough, but we lose access to our deeper intelligence—the creative, spiritual, and emotional wisdom that fuels the ability to take center stage of our lives!

When we adopt an NPC mindset, we outsource our agency. We absorb beliefs, follow expectations, and respond to life's demands without questioning their origin. Growth, however, requires presence. It demands choice. It asks us to become conscious of the narratives we've inherited, the roles we've accepted, and the identities we've outgrown. When you stop living like a background character and start acting like a soul with purpose, the world opens up, and so do you.

You are not an NPC in your own life. You are the main character, the one who shapes the story. But if you surround yourself with people who discourage growth, roll their eyes at ambition, or project their fears onto you, you risk becoming a background character in someone else's story.

It's easy to say, "Don't listen to the naysayers." But what happens when the naysayer is someone you love? A close friend, a family member, or even a spouse? Sometimes the people we expect to support us the most turn out to be the dragons we must face head-on. And that's painful. We want their validation. We want them to believe in us. But if they don't, we must make a decision: Do we let their doubt become our reality, or do we push forward anyway?

Having true depth of character means standing firm in your convictions, even when it's unpopular. It means not engaging in petty back-and-forth conversations, not defending yourself to those committed to misunderstanding you. When someone underestimates you, let them. Then prove them wrong by your results.

Relationships, whether familial or chosen, require discernment. Ask yourself:

- Do they lift me up or tear me down?

- Do they challenge me in a way that fosters growth, or in a way that makes me doubt myself?

- Do I feel drained after interacting with them, or am I energized?

The company you keep will either propel you forward or keep you stagnant. Choose wisely.

Discernment is Your Superpower

Not every battle is worth fighting. Not every comment needs a rebuttal. Some people thrive on conflict, and engaging with them only steals your peace. Learn the art of moving on. High-achieving women—the movers and shakers of the world—do not waste energy rehashing every slight, every rude comment, every dig disguised as a joke. They recognize that not everything deserves a reaction. Does this mean you should tolerate disrespect? Absolutely not. But it does mean recognizing when to walk away, when to set boundaries, and when to let your success be the loudest response.

As moms, as women, as individuals with dreams, our plans can get buried under daily responsibilities. Homework, piles of laundry, work deadlines, dinner prep—it's easy to get stuck in the cycle of survive/repeat. If you don't make time for your dreams, no one else will. You have to be intentional. You have to carve out time. Maybe it's fifteen minutes before the kids wake up. Maybe it's a late-night writing session. Maybe it's saying no to one extra obligation so you can say yes to yourself. If you don't, the noise of life (the distractions, the doubt, the negativity) will drown out what truly matters.

REFLECTIONS

1. A dream I've been hesitant to share because I fear judgment is

_____.

2. The person or thing that most distracts me from my goals is

_____.

3. A time when I let someone else's doubt hold me back was

_____.

4. I feel most confident in my dreams when I

_____.

5. One way I can guard my dreams better is by

_____.

6. The people who truly support me and my goals are

_____.

7. One belief I need to let go of in order to move forward is

_____.

8. If I fully believed in myself, the first thing I would do is

_____.

TAKEAWAYS

- Identify the people who lift you up and those who drain you.

- Limit how much access negative voices have to your dreams.

- Surround yourself with those who challenge and inspire you.

- Be intentional about protecting your time and energy.

- Take action. Even small steps compound into big change.

The world is full of noise. It will try to tell you who to be, what to do, and how far you can go. You get to decide if you listen. Remember, at the end of the day, the only voice that matters is *your voice*. Let it be strong. Let it be clear. And let it guide you to the center stage of your life.

Chapter Eighteen

Burying Excuses

We have more ability than willpower, and it is often an excuse to ourselves that we imagine that things are impossible.

—François de la Rochefoucauld

Excuses do not deserve a simple flush down the drain. They need to be buried six feet under, never to rise again. For every reason why you should chase a goal, there is an excuse whispering why you shouldn't. Which voice are you listening to? You might feel like there's an angel and a devil on each shoulder every time you make a move. That inner debate? It's a sign you're on to something big. If you weren't taking action, there wouldn't be a battle in your mind at all.

So what are you going to do? Keep letting that inner critic dictate your future? Or silence it once and for all? Because every step forward will turn into two steps back if you keep entertaining the doubts, fears, and limiting beliefs that whisper, *You're not ready. You're not good enough. You'll fail again.*

And maybe, deep down, that's exactly what you believe. Maybe you've put off setting big goals, calling that client, getting your coaching license, or taking the leap because somewhere inside, you don't think you're worthy of success. If failure has kept you frozen, it's time to flip the lens. Failure is a damn good teacher. You will always learn more from your fails than from your wins. So instead of carrying failure like a weight on your back, use it as a blueprint for what comes next. You already know which mistakes not to do. You've earned every insight through trial and error. Even if you pivot in a completely new direction, your experiences still serve you. But you must make a choice: Bury the failure. Keep the lessons. Move forward.

Beyond Excuses

My youngest child has had an IEP since elementary school. It started with delayed speech and a struggle to grasp certain developmental skills that other kids seemed to pick up effortlessly. For years, even something as simple as knowing which shoe went on which foot (or tying his laces) felt like climbing a mountain. And not everyone is kind to a child with needs that aren't visible on the surface.

I remember taking him rock climbing when he was young. I watched as he stood there, trying to process where to place each foot, his mind taking a beat longer to decode what came so naturally to other kids. It was painful to watch. If I could have taken that challenge away and carried it for him, I would have done it in a heartbeat.

In my pain for him, I was tempted to bark back at people who so easily gave their opinions on what was wrong with him, what I needed to do, and why these delays were occurring. But I didn't respond with excuses and reasons why. I didn't overcompensate by coddling him. And believe me, I could have swooped in, made life easier for him, and shielded him from every unkind word or comparison. My son could have chosen to give up when reaching developmental milestones felt too difficult. But he never did. He never said, "I can't . . ." Instead, he wanted to try, to test his abilities, to endure.

As mothers, we want to fix what hurts. We want to move every mountain for our child. And when we can't, we find ways around it. We search, we ask, we experiment. That's what I did. I left no stone unturned. Honestly, I hesitated writing about this. But I know someone out there needs to hear it. Someone needs to feel the hope that I clung to in those dark moments.

We tried so many things. To this day, I'm not sure we ever landed on the exact diagnosis. But I've come to understand it was likely a processing issue. Imagine having a conversation where someone fires off four rapid prompts while you're still mentally decoding the first. That's what it was like for my son. At first, we tried soccer. Everyone said it would help. But it didn't click. He seemed confused, lost in the game. In his efforts to keep up, he became overwhelmed. One day, his kindergarten teacher suggested taekwondo, which changed everything. That, along with drums and Kumon, became our lifeline. It didn't happen overnight. He spent years in slow, quiet progress. But from the beginning, I knew my boy was going to rise.

I taught him affirmations that he still recites today. I worked alongside him toward every small win. He went from the kid who struggled to the kid who became resilient, disciplined, focused, and fierce. And most people never knew the battles he was fighting because I did the work in the background, speaking life over him, creating systems that nurtured him. I knew the power of what I was instilling. That's the thing about solutions; they come when you face your challenges head-on.

Now he's in middle school. And guess what? I don't have to remind him to do anything. He comes home, goes straight to his computer, and gets to work. He studies in intervals like I taught him, and I quiz him for exams. He memorizes everything. And he aces his tests. The last year has brought him the most growth, being on the straight-A honor roll often. Right now, as I type this, my boy has all As and one B—and all of his classes are advanced or accelerated. I'm beyond proud—not just because of the grades, but because I saw the journey. I witnessed the struggle. I sat in the waiting rooms, asked the questions, and stood in the fire with him.

Mothers have powerful intuition. You know your child. You feel things others can't see. And while you don't need to shout it from the rooftops, you do have a sacred responsibility to empower and guide them. That's what I did. I protected my son's space while he grew through his adversity. And grow he did—with resilience, confidence and fight.

Use Excuses as Fuel

What if, instead of excuses holding you back, they propelled you forward? Let's try something radical: Reverse-engineer your success. Instead of working toward your goals and hoping to reach them someday, start embodying success now.

- Dress like the version of you who has already arrived.

- Speak with the confidence of someone who knows they belong in the room.

- Show up every day like the person you aspire to become.

This is about training your mind to believe in your own power. When you start seeing yourself as capable, worthy, and embodying that elevated version of you—not just *wishing* to be her—you start acting accordingly.

Trying to be the next [*insert successful person here*]? It's a waste of time. You'll always be second-best at being someone else but first place at being you. Yes, study the habits of successful people. Learn from them. But add your own spin. You weren't made to be a knockoff version of someone else. You were uniquely handcrafted.

There is no other you on this planet. Your voice is one of a kind. Your perspective is uniquely yours. Your skills, your experiences, your story—no one else has that combination. So why shrink yourself into someone else's mold? Why dim your light to fit into a space that wasn't designed for you? Step into your power. Own your magic. Then put that magic to work. Because no amount of self-talk and manifestation will replace action.

I've met countless people who talk big about their dreams that *could* change their lives. But that's all they do. *Talk.* And after years of talking and no action, guess what? People stop listening. If you've been caught in that cycle—*bury it.* Excuses, inaction, and procrastination will not bring you closer to the life you want. What will? Doing the work.

Lack of Time and Money Excuses

I won't sit here and tell you that time and money are not real barriers. They are. But I will tell you that they are not insurmountable. Let's put it to the test. Write out your daily schedule hour by hour. Track what you do from the moment you wake up to the moment you go to sleep. Then analyze it:

- What are your biggest time-wasters?

- Where can you cut back or replace mindless habits with goal-driven action?

- What small shifts could free up space for what matters?

Now, look at your finances. What's one step you can take right now that doesn't cost a fortune? When I began providing marketing services to small and medium-sized companies, my first paid gig was for my oldest son's preschool: $150. That was it. From there, my next client paid me at least eight times that amount. Today, I charge thousands for a single project. Did I start with the best tools? No. I used the free version of Canva. I taught myself to build websites from scratch. I bought $100 courses and learned.

If I had told myself, "I don't have the money to invest in my business," I never would have started. Instead, I worked with what I had and leveled up along the way. The truth? Excuses are a cop-out. There is always a way forward if you're willing to get creative, get resourceful, and get moving.

The "Not Right Now" Lie

How many times have you said, "Now is not the right time"? And when will the right time be? Life will always be busy. The timing will never be perfect. There will always be responsibilities, distractions, and obstacles. You could wait for the "perfect" moment, or you could just start with the first step right now, no matter how small.

Highly successful people don't wait for perfect conditions. They create them. They delegate. They prioritize. They find a way. If you don't have hired help, get creative. Can you carve out an hour a day? Can you adjust your routine? If you really want it, you will find a way.

If you don't do the hard things first, you won't do them at all. My youngest son already understands this. He does his homework the second he walks through the door without procrastinating. That's why he is always prepared. That's why he never scrambles at the last minute. Now imagine if you applied that same discipline to your goals. Want to be a writer? Write every day. Want to be a fitness coach? Train like one. Want to build a business? Start learning, networking, and putting yourself out there.

Be "Her" Before You Arrive

Your vision—the one swirling in your mind, the one keeping you up at night—is waiting to be acted upon. But no one else will do it for you. You don't need to have all the answers. You don't need a detailed blueprint. You just need to start showing up as her—the woman who already lives that vision. Walk like her. Speak like her. Decide like her. Move like her. Because when you embody the version of you that already exists in your heart, the path begins to rise to meet your feet.

Faith is believing before the evidence appears. Go. Bury the excuses. Start building the life you were meant to live. Be her—*now,* not later. Act as if you've already achieved your goal. Answer these questions as if you've already arrived: How does the successful you show up daily? What habits, mindset, and actions define this version of yourself? How do you speak about yourself and your work?

Write a paragraph in present tense describing your life as if your goal has already been achieved. For Example: "I am a thriving entrepreneur with a growing business. My schedule is full of purposeful tasks, and I make time for what truly matters. I speak with confidence because I know my value. I no longer let fear dictate my actions. I take bold steps daily toward my vision."

Pick one hard thing that you've been putting off—something that makes you uncomfortable but will move you closer to your goal. Then do it. Send that email. Make that call. Write the first page. Film the video. Post the content. Whatever it is, rip off the Band-Aid and take the first step today.

REFLECTIONS

The "No More Excuses" Letter

Write a letter to your future self—the version of you who has already succeeded.

"Dear [Your Name], I am so proud of you. You finally stopped making excuses and went all in on your dreams. Here's what happened when you did . . ."

Describe everything you achieved. How has your life changed? How does it feel to have buried your excuses for good? Seal it in an envelope and then set a reminder to open it in six months.

The Excuse Burial Exercise

1. Write down the top-three excuses that have been holding you back. Be brutally honest.

- "I don't have enough time."
- "I'm not experienced enough to start."
- "I'm afraid I'll fail (again)."

2. For each excuse, flip the script. Rewrite them as empowering truths:

- "I will make time by restructuring my day and cutting out time-wasters."

- "No one starts as an expert. Learning as I go is part of the process."

- "Every failure is a step closer to success. I can't win if I don't try."

Then, physically destroy the excuses. Rip them up. Burn them (safely). Bury them in your backyard. Throw them in the trash. Do something symbolic to reinforce the idea that these excuses no longer control you.

TAKEAWAYS

- *Excuses are the enemy of progress:* Excuses might feel valid in the moment, but they're often fear in disguise. Every time you let one slide, you hand over the wheel to your inner critic. True growth starts when you recognize that the only thing standing between you and your goals is the narrative you keep repeating.

- *Your struggles can become your strengths:* Whether it's your own journey or your child's, adversity can be the training ground for resilience. Watching my son rise through his challenges is a reminder that perseverance, not perfection, builds character, and that progress often comes from the quiet work no one sees.

- *Stop waiting for the perfect moment:* There will never be a "perfect time." Life will always be busy, messy, and unpredictable. If you keep waiting, you'll be stuck in the same place six months from now. Start before you're ready. The act of doing creates clarity.

- *Embody your vision now:* Don't wait until the goal is achieved to start acting like the version of you who made it. Show up with the energy, confidence, and mindset of the woman who already lives her dream. When you believe differently, you behave differently.

● *Use failure as a blueprint, not a burial ground:* Failure doesn't mean you should stop. Instead, see it as a chance to learn. Let it teach you what didn't work so you can refine your path forward. Your most valuable lessons often come from your hardest falls.

● *Rituals make change real:* Symbolic actions like writing a "No More Excuses" letter help make internal shifts tangible. These practices reinforce your decision to change and also remind you that you are done playing small.

Chapter Nineteen

Empty Nester*ism*

Letting go of our children is the most sacrificial way we can love them. Make no mistake, to hold on too tight and too long clips their wings and makes it harder for them to fly. To soar.
—Robin Dance

My twelve-year-old son is practicing his black belt forms, moving with a grace and purpose that stop me in my tracks. His arms slice the air with precision, his movements a fierce dance of discipline and confidence. Watching him, I'm suddenly transported back to the beginning (his first-grade year) when this journey started. There were so many moments he wanted to quit, days when the training felt too long, too hard. But he kept going. Sometimes with my encouragement, sometimes

211

with my push. And now, here he is: steady, focused, and strong.

By contrast, my older son's path has looked completely different. He's always been sharp—one of those kids who could grasp things quickly, often without trying too hard. For a while, he coasted on that natural ability. Schoolwork came easily. Challenges weren't frequent, so he didn't always see the value in pushing himself. But, focus was a struggle. I could see he had the potential, but he wasn't fully tapping into it. And if I'm honest, it was hard to watch sometimes.

But then something started to shift. At age fourteen, he began working at Publix, bagging and carting groceries. It wasn't glamorous, but it taught him discipline, accountability, and how to show up consistently. I knew that job would spark immense growth. It became the catalyst for his growth. That responsibility, combined with the natural tug of growing older, began reshaping him.

Now he's sixteen, and I'm in awe. His maturity has taken a front seat. His conversations have profound depth. He's become more intentional with his time, his grades, and his vision for the future. To my delight, he is currently enrolled in a Cambridge-recognized program and is excelling. He's researching his future without me nudging him, exploring what steps he needs to take to pursue the life he wants.

It's not that life suddenly became easier. It's that he stepped up. He decided to own his future. The same boy who used to get distracted now carries himself with bold confidence. And although he exuded confidence prior to the growth, this confidence has permeated his posture, his speech patterns, and his interactions. I see a young man forming—driven not by pressure, but by purpose. And I'm watching with so much pride, knowing he's just getting started.

This is what it looks like when our kids begin to outgrow us. When they start becoming themselves. As mothers, we pour everything we have into raising our children—our time, our energy, our entire identities. We guide, protect, and prepare. But no one really prepares us for the moment when we must begin to let go. The shift happens quietly. A little more independence here. A little less hand-holding there. And then one day, they simply don't need us the same way anymore. It's beautiful. And heartbreaking. It is pride laced with a quiet ache. But if we are paying attention, we will see that their growth invites our own.

Identity Shift: From Mom to More

When the kids leave, it's not just their rooms that become empty. There is a part of you that is gone too. For years, your identity has been woven into theirs, your purpose tied to their needs. Now the silence is deafening. And you're left staring into the quiet asking, "Who am I without them?"

This empty nest feels like a void. A gaping space where your sense of purpose once thrived. And as brutal as that realization can be, it's also a call. A raw invitation to meet the woman who has been waiting under the layers of motherhood. What passions did you bury under routines and school calendars? What dreams did you defer? This is the moment to stop hiding behind to-do lists and start unearthing the you who has been whispering ideas for years.

In this phase of life, you are not starting from scratch but can draw from your vast experience. It won't be easy. There will be nights you ache for the noise and chaos of growing kids. But there is a new woman emerging. Not just a mom. It's you as a woman, independent from the label of mother. You are like a hologram that changes with the shift in perspective. You are bold, curious, unapologetically whole.

Embracing Change and Growth

The universe just handed you a blank canvas. That familiar rhythm is gone, and the house hums with stillness. It can feel disorienting, but it's also electric with possibility.

Confront the Stillness

Your old routines are gone. The hustle is over. Now you get to ask: "What do I want my days to look like?" Sit with the discomfort. In that silence, listen for what stirs you. Often, the things you've buried the deepest are the ones worth resurrecting.

Dust off the Dreams

What has been tugging at your spirit? That art class, the book idea, the trail you wanted to hike? This is your time to follow curiosity wherever it leads. Let it stretch you. Let it surprise you.

Get Comfortable with the Unfamiliar

Growth is never cozy. But you're not fragile; you're forged. Lean into the newness. Let change sharpen you. There is no "too late" when it comes to becoming.

Writing the Next Chapter

Your story is just getting better. This is the chapter where you stop living for everyone else and start living fully for you. How? Surround yourself with kindred spirits. Find people who reflect your new energy. Women who are reinventing themselves. People who challenge you and see you not just as "mom" but as someone rising.

Honor your layers. You're not discarding motherhood or deleting your past; you're building upon it. Every tear, triumph, and tired night has shaped you. Let it empower the woman you're becoming. But emotional resilience is your secret weapon. Feel everything. Stop numbing. Stop pretending. Cry if you need to. Get angry. Laugh at how absurd and beautiful this season is. Don't push emotions away; meet them head-on. That's where the healing starts.

Silence the inner critic. When those creeping doubts arrive—*Did I do enough? Am I still needed?*—shut them down. Replace the noise with truth: "I am still becoming. I am worthy even without being needed nonstop."

Find connection. Text your best friend. Join the group. Book the therapy session. You don't have to muscle through this alone. Human connection heals in ways no book or podcast ever could. Then adapt. Pivot. Rise. Life will throw curveballs. Plans will unravel. But adaptability is your superpower. Bend. Shift. Keep going. There is beauty in being fluid like water. You are unstoppable.

Redefining Your Nest

The term "empty nest" makes it sound like something has been lost. But what if, instead, something is gained? When your children leave, it's not just their absence that reshapes your world; it's the quiet invitation to come home to yourself. See that extra room as a possibility. Paint it, fill it with music, write your story, stretch your limbs and your life. This is your home, and now it can reflect the woman you've become: wild, wise, and still hungry for more.

Your time is yours again. After years of running on other people's schedules, you finally get to ask yourself: *What do I want to do today?* You can learn the language you once said you didn't have time for, launch the business you dreamed about in the carpool line, or book the solo trip that used to feel out of reach. The freedom is real. And you've earned every ounce of it.

And while your role as mother will never change, your relationship with your children can evolve into something even deeper. You're still their anchor, but now you're also a mentor, a muse, a trusted voice they return to not because they have to, but because they want to. Keep the emotional door open. Let your bond expand into this new season.

Yes, the unknown can feel unsettling. But within it lies magic. Let curiosity lead you. Say yes to what you don't yet understand. Because your next chapter isn't written, and that's exactly what makes it so full of potential.

REFLECTIONS

~Personal Milestones~

What defining moments have shaped you outside of motherhood?

_____

_____

How did they help you become who you are today?

_____

_____

~Future Aspirations~

What have you always wanted to do but put on hold to raise a family?

_____

_____

What is one step you can take toward your dream this month?

_____

_____

~Evolving Identity~

Who are you becoming in this season?

_____

_____

What parts of yourself are being reawakened?

_____

_____

~Gratitude Reflection~

What are you grateful for during this transition?

_____

_____

How can gratitude help shift your perspective?

_____

_____

A portal is opening. You are just beginning. What you will see ahead is bigger, bolder, and more authentically *you* than ever before.

TAKEAWAYS

• *Feel it all*: Let the emotions rise: grief, relief, joy. Don't judge them. Let them pass through you.

• *Reconnect with your partner*: If you are partnered, now is the time to rediscover each other. Explore new things. Reignite the passion that has been dormant.

• *Pursue your passion projects*: That thing you always said you would do someday? Do it now.

• *Redefine the bond with your kids*: Stay connected without clinging. Trust them to fly, and trust yourself to soar too.

• *Seek support*: If it gets heavy, reach out for therapy or coaching. Circles of women going through the same thing. You are not alone.

Chapter Twenty

Bucket List

Twenty years from now you will be more disappointed by the things that you didn't do than by the ones you did do. So throw off the bowlines. Sail away from the safe harbor. Catch the trade winds in your sails. Explore. Dream. Discover.

—Mark Twain

What will your future self say about the life you have lived? Will she remember the adventures? The soft breeze of the Amalfi Coast, the thrill of standing under the Eiffel Tower, the sound of your children laughing in a cabin in the mountains, the long walk to the temple in Bali, the book you wrote, the stories you told? Or will she mourn the dreams you buried?

Are you holding dreams inside that you've written off as too big, too wild? Or dreams that you brushed off and thought, *Maybe in another life*? But here's the truth: If it still lives inside you, it's not dead. It's simply dormant. And dormant dreams are just waiting for you to wake them the hell up.

Reawakening Dormant Dreams

Life is heavy. Kids, bills, aging parents, careers. Somewhere between soccer practice and endless spreadsheets, your own dreams get shelved. You tell yourself you'll circle back "someday." But the thing about someday is that it's a sneaky little thief. It disappears unless you grab it by the collar and make it today.

Remember the Ice Bucket Challenge? People all over the world dumped freezing water over their heads to raise awareness for ALS. Yes, it was a social media trend, but it also broke people out of their comfort zones. For a moment, we remembered what it felt like to do something that jolted us awake.

That's what your bucket list should do—shake you up. Make you feel alive again. Push you toward the things that have been whispering to you for years. A bucket list is a personal manifesto. It reflects intentional living. It's your rebellion against living on autopilot. A bucket list can help you:

- Reconnect with your passions, the things that light you up from the inside.

- Break the cycle of monotony, introducing awe, joy, and spontaneity into your world.

- Feel damn proud because checking something off that list just hits different.

One of my own bucket list dreams was writing a book. For years, it sat in the background of my life—this quiet ache, this whisper I kept ignoring. I was too busy. Too uncertain. Too overwhelmed with life and motherhood to believe I had the time or the voice. But the desire didn't go away. It tugged at me in the quiet moments when I was folding laundry or stuck in traffic. It resurfaced after hard seasons—whenever I questioned who I was beyond everyone else's needs. So I finally said yes. Writing this book was terrifying, thrilling, healing. It reminded me of who I am. It gave me permission to dream again, not just about writing, but about living more boldly. That's what bucket list dreams do. They redefine you.

Real-Life Legends

John Goddard, American adventurer and explorer, when he was fifteen, overheard adults complaining about their regrets. So he made a list of 127 bold, wild goals: climbing peaks, studying cultures, exploring the world's great rivers. He ended up achieving over one hundred of them. His life became a masterclass in living with intention.

Dorothy Smith, at age 102, visited her final continent—Australia—with the help of her family and the Yes Theory YouTube crew. She stood in front of the Sydney Opera House and walked Bondi Beach. Proof that it's never too late. The clock doesn't decide when your dreams expire. You do.

REFLECTIONS

My Bold Bucket List

A list of dreams await you. Mark an X when you've done it. Let your "why this dream matters" prompt remind you of your *why*.

Done ✔	Bucket List Item	Why This Dream Matters

It's not too late. You're right on time. This season (right now) is an invitation to dream again. Not just daydream, but *take action*. Let this be the moment you say yes to what lights you up inside.

Start by giving yourself the gift of quiet. Just a few uninterrupted minutes to ask: *What do I still want to experience?* Think big. Think bold. Think about adventure, creativity, love, legacy. Let the questions stir something awake in you. Now, write it down. Ten things you want to do, see, or create in this lifetime. Don't worry if it feels too big or too small. If it matters to you, it belongs on the list.

Then, look at your list—not with logic, but with your heart. Which one tugs at you the most? Which dream makes your eyes light up? That's your starting point. Pick one and begin shaping it. Break it into tiny, doable steps. Choose a date. Circle it. Make it real. Keep your dream where you can see it—taped to your mirror, tucked in your journal, saved as your phone wallpaper. Let it remind you that life is not just passing you by; it's waiting for you to join in.

Take one bold step. Today. Book the flight. Sign up for the class. Reach out to that person. One move can change everything. As you go, document the journey. Write about it. Speak it into voice notes. Snap the pictures. Not just for the memories, but to watch your own transformation unfold.

And when you finally check it off? Don't just move on. Celebrate it. Sit with the version of yourself who made it happen. Reflect on what it took, who you became, and what you're ready to pursue next. Your list is a reflection of your becoming.

TAKEAWAYS

- *Proactive pursuit*: Bucket lists make dreams tangible and achievable.

- *Personal growth*: Bold goals stretch you. And that stretch becomes strength.

- *Intentional living*: This is your roadmap to joy, not just productivity.

- *Evolving vision*: You get to edit, add, delete. Just don't stop dreaming.

- *Legacy creation*: Your list becomes a life story—one worth telling, one worth living.

Don't wait for the "right" time. Make now the right time. Let your bucket list be your permission slip to go after the life that has been waiting for you to wake up and want it.

Chapter Twenty One

The Problem with Good Enough

I alone cannot change the world, but I can cast a stone across the water to create many ripples.

—Mother Teresa

Throughout history, women have been haunted by the insidious whisper of inadequacy. We've all questioned our worthiness, doubted our right to chase audacious dreams, and wondered if we truly deserve the visions plastered on our vision boards. Society groomed boys to dominate boardrooms and ascend to CEO status, while girls were conditioned to be compliant, their ambitions stifled by double standards and societal shame.

I recall a vivid memory from my teenage years. At fourteen, I took a bus to the bustling market—a cherished pastime in my hometown. There, I bumped into a boy I knew with striking long hair, piercing green eyes, and a smile that could light up the darkest room. We chatted innocently, but fate had other plans. An auntie spotted us and hurried to inform my mother, proclaiming I had a "boyfriend." Suddenly, I (a total goodie two-shoes) was thrust into a position where I had to defend a harmless conversation. Growing up in a strict environment, morality was policed by societal norms. Extended interactions with boys? Scandalous. Cutting one's hair? Rebellious. Voicing an opinion as a child? Unthinkable. These rigid expectations taught us girls to be silent, to suppress our voices. While I believe in setting boundaries, such oppressive standards only serve to diminish a girl's spirit. As a mother to boys, I strive to raise them as respectful, bold, and confident individuals. Our daughters deserve the same empowerment.

These societal constraints seep into our psyche, planting seeds of self-doubt. We find ourselves asking, "Am I worth it? Am I good enough?" Yes, you are! You were designed for greatness, achieved through persistent, sometimes monotonous steps. Your future self will thank you for the efforts you invest today. You've likely extended countless chances to others—the partner who repeatedly hurts you, the friend who manipulates situations. We distribute these chances freely, like coupons. So why not grant yourself the same grace? Why not take a chance on you?

Perhaps you believe that daring dreams are reserved for others—for those who have already "made it." You admire their confidence, their perceived worth, yet you undervalue your own unique talents and creativity. But you are skilled. Reflect on how adeptly you navigate your life. There is ample room in any arena you wish to enter. Countless others may have walked the path, but none have done it your way. Your perspective is unparalleled. Embrace the ingenuity that comes from being authentically you.

Lean into Your Ugly

Sometimes it gets ugly before things turn beautiful. Native to the Middle East, particularly Syria, the Damascus goat is renowned for its dramatic transformation as it matures. As kids, these goats have charming features: long, floppy ears and delicate faces that many find endearing. But as they grow, their appearance shifts dramatically. Adults develop a pronounced "Roman nose" and lose some of their soft features, leading many to call them unattractive by conventional standards. Yet in places like Syria and Cyprus, these goats are prized. Their uniqueness isn't mocked but celebrated. They win beauty contests *because* of this transformation. Beyond their looks, they are known for their high milk yield, adaptability, and resilience.

That journey from adorable to awkward to exceptional is the metaphor. Transformation isn't always pretty. Growth often looks like chaos. But what others may call ugly might just be the price of becoming powerful, valuable, and one-of-a-kind.

Beginnings are messy. You will question yourself. You'll look in the mirror and not recognize who you're becoming. That's part of it. We've been conditioned to chase perfection, but perfection is a myth. What's real is progress. What's real is the grit it takes to keep showing up. Excellence is earned—step by step, choice by choice.

My mother exemplified this truth. She ran a business in the local market, and we were all enlisted to help. She was the original boss—a force to be reckoned with. I stood outside the shop, attempting to lure potential customers, especially during the frenetic Christmas season. The market teemed with people, and vendors vied for attention, hoping to sell their wares. The pulse in the air was electric with noise and motion, alive with the shouts of vendors and the shuffle of feet as people wove through tight, crowded aisles, arms loaded with goods. The heat was suffocating—thick, wet air pressed against my skin, sweat slid down my back faster than I could wipe it away. The scent of spices, ripe fruit, and sun-baked concrete clung to everything. In that kind of heat, every task felt doubled: not only did you have to show up—you had to perform. Smile. Speak. Sell. Be convincing. Be unbothered. And my mother? She didn't flinch. She faced it all— abominable heat, sweat, pressure—with her sleeves rolled up and a look that said, *Let's go.* She didn't wait for conditions to be perfect. She did the work. And she did it with gusto.

As a child, she would wake me at four a.m., bathing me on the veranda before embarking on a grueling journey to the city. That wasn't particularly enjoyable, but what she did for rest of the day reduced bathing with frigid water to child's play. Mom traveled for hours (by bus, boat, and car) to procure merchandise for the shop. We lacked the luxury of a car, so she navigated this arduous trek regularly. Upon returning, she rose early the next day to sort and price goods. Our shop's shutters weren't the convenient metal roll-ups found in malls; they were heavy wooden panels that required manual assembly each morning and disassembly each evening. My mother tackled this laborious routine without complaint. I watched in awe as she transformed tragedy into tenacity, rebuilding her life after my father's untimely death. Her resilience, forged in our homeland of Guyana, molded her into the formidable woman I admire today.

The Mental Game

Success is largely a mental battle. A resilient mind can weather any storm; a fragile one crumbles under pressure. My mental fortitude is a product of my upbringing. I view challenges as difficult but surmountable; nothing is impossible. This mindset stems from self-belief and a positive outlook. That's not to say I don't experience anger or frustration; I do. But I refuse to let negativity linger. I move forward swiftly, eschewing drama and striving to treat everyone with kindness. Confidence is born from embodying patience and compassion. When you're known for these qualities, you attract positivity and repel toxicity.

I firmly believe in minding my own business and tending to my responsibilities. Evaluate the quality of your relationships—both personal and professional. Your role in others' lives reflects the value you bring. By assessing our interactions, you gain clarity on your contributions and can navigate relationships with greater understanding.

Building meaningful connections requires effort. Genuine friendships, strong marriages, and healthy family bonds don't materialize out of thin air; they are cultivated through dedication. I don't expect kindness if I project rudeness. I don't anticipate referrals if I neglect my clients. My mental resilience is a byproduct of my approach to life. Each day, I rise with gratitude, recognizing the gift of a new day. I greet challenges with a smile, ready to offer my best self. Those who lead with integrity and authenticity are mentally robust. They honor their commitments, acknowledge mistakes, and earn respect by giving it freely. If you demand respect without offering it, you'll find it elusive. Life operates on reciprocity: For every action, there is a reaction. The universe responds to our deeds and intentions accordingly.

The Power of Intentional Consumption

Our minds are constantly bombarded with information, much of which subtly shapes our perceptions, self-worth, and aspirations. The content we consume—be it through social media, news outlets, or entertainment—acts as the diet for our minds. Just as a steady intake of junk food can deteriorate our physical health, consuming negative or superficial content can erode our mental well-being and sense of self.

Feeding your mind with enriching content is akin to fueling your body with nutritious food. It builds resilience, fosters a positive self-image, and propels you toward your goals. By consciously choosing what you allow into your mental space, you reclaim agency over your self-worth and aspirations.

Embrace Lifelong Learning

Reflecting on my own path, I've found that stepping beyond traditional academia into the realm of self-directed learning has been transformative. Engaging with diverse books, exploring new concepts, and enrolling in various courses have not only expanded my knowledge but also ignited a passion for personal growth.

Equally impactful has been the practice of consistent, positive self-talk. By consciously replacing negative thoughts with affirmations, I have cultivated a mindset that embraces challenges and fosters resilience. This combination of continuous learning and affirming self-dialogue has been instrumental in shaping a more confident and empowered version of myself. Remember, you are the gatekeeper of your mind. Nourish it with content that empowers and uplifts, and watch as your perception of "good enough" transforms into a relentless pursuit of your fullest potential.

REFLECTIONS

Reclaiming Your Worth

Exercise #1

"GOOD ENOUGH" Moments

Think back to three specific moments in your life where you settled for good enough. Maybe it was in a relationship, a job, your health, or a personal goal. What made you settle? What were you afraid of?

Write them down:

- Moment 1:

_____

- Moment 2:

_____

- Moment 3:

_____

Now, beside each one, answer: What would my life look like if I believed I deserved better?

Exercise #2

THE "WHAT IF I DON'T SETTLE?" VISUALIZATION

Close your eyes and imagine the version of yourself who never settles due to your clarity, confidence, and courage.

- What does she do differently?
- How does she speak?
- How does she handle setbacks?
- What kinds of people does she attract?
- What goals does she chase?

Now write a paragraph describing her in present tense: *"I am the woman who . . ."*

Exercise #3

YOUR MENTAL DIET AUDIT

On the left side of the page, list five types of content (accounts, shows, podcasts, people, environments) you consume regularly.

On the right side, write how each one makes you feel— empowered or drained?

Content I Consume	How It Makes Me Feel

Circle one you need to release. Star one you want more of.

Exercise #4

THE "I AM BECOMING" LIST

List five affirmations that reflect who you're becoming, not who you've been. Begin each with *"I am becoming..."*

Examples:

- I am becoming a woman who honors her voice.

- I am becoming someone who shows up with boldness.

241

Exercise #5

ONE BRAVE ACTION

What is one thing you've been holding back on out of fear that you're "not ready" or "not enough"? Write it down. Then underneath it, finish this sentence: *"Even if I feel scared, I will take one step by . . ."*

Bonus Idea: Seal this in an envelope or journal it digitally with a reminder to revisit in ninety days. Let this be your proof that you didn't just read this chapter; you acted on it.

TAKEAWAYS

- *Mindful consumption*: The information you engage with daily influences your self-perception and aspirations.

- *Intentional learning*: Pursuing knowledge beyond formal education fosters personal growth and resilience.

- *Positive self-talk*: Replacing negative thoughts with affirmations enhances confidence and motivation.

- *Curate your media intake*: Choose content that inspires and educates.

- *Set boundaries*: Limit exposure to negative or superficial information.

- *Engage in lifelong learning*: Dedicate time to read, take courses, or explore new skills.

- *Practice positive affirmations*: Incorporate daily affirmations to reinforce self-belief.

Chapter Twenty Two

Incognito

Faith and fear both demand you believe in something you cannot see. You choose!
—Bob Proctor

There is something powerful about hiding in plain sight. Not in a fearful, shrinking way. But in a sovereign, strategic, self-preserving sense. I'm talking about the kind of incognito that lets you move without explanation, make power moves without announcing your plans, and pull away from the noise without guilt.

Sometimes you have to disappear to show up for yourself. And no, that doesn't always mean booking a retreat in Bali. Sometimes it's as small as putting your phone on silent and turning down the volume of the world so you can finally hear your own thoughts. The world will drain you dry if you let it. The kids. The partner. The boss. The business. The group chat. The fake urgency of a million little notifications. Everyone wants a piece of you, and they expect access like you owe them your energy on demand.

You don't owe anyone. But you do owe YOU. You owe yourself the silence, the mystery, the sacred pause. You owe yourself the right to not explain everything. Going incognito is not avoidance. It's reclamation. It's the quiet rebellion of a woman who has realized her peace is too precious to be negotiated in public.

I used to feel guilty when I pulled back. When I didn't return calls. When I didn't show up to every birthday brunch or reply to every text. I used to think being low-key was selfish. That going ghost-mode meant I was a bad friend, a bad mom, or a bad woman. But now I know better. I know that presence means nothing when you feel exhausted, resentful, and stretched so thin you're only showing up as a fraction of yourself.

Now I disappear on purpose. Sometimes for a weekend. Sometimes for weeks. I delete apps. I clear my calendar. I pour into me. And when I return I come back clearer. Sharper. Grounded. That's the thing about going incognito. You vanish because you're about to be found by yourself.

Going incognito is a conscious decision to *unplug* so you can *reconnect* with your desires, your purpose, your next chapter. Not everything needs an audience. You don't have to make an announcement every time you choose yourself. You are allowed to move in silence and let your healing, your glow-up, your next level speak for itself.

Disappearing for a while does not mean you want to be invisible. It means you are self- protecting, preparing. It's your time to go into the cocoon before the comeback. So the next time you feel like retreating, ask yourself: *Do I want to hide or heal?* This silence is an intentional consciousness. A form of clarity. It's about vanishing long enough to remember that you're powerful. It's what happens when you realize your energy is sacred, and not everyone deserves front-row access to your unfolding.

The old version of you may have thought being available nonstop made you worthy. That your value was tied to how reachable, responsive, and reliable you were for everyone else but yourself. But there comes a moment (a mirror moment) when you realize the version of you that's always on is running on fumes. You catch a glimpse of your own reflection and hardly recognize the woman staring back. She is exhausted from doing too much and being too much.

So you pull back out of reverence. For yourself. For your journey. For your becoming. That's what incognito really is: an act of reverence. A bowing out so you can rise again. And here is the truth most won't admit: Some of your most powerful moves will be made in this silence. No validation. No cosign. No applause.

Not every seed sprouts in public. Some transformations are too sacred for the spotlight. This is your reminder that it's okay to be unseen while you rebuild. To be unheard while you realign. The cocoon is a consecration. And when you reemerge, you will be rested and resurrected. Sharper. Lighter. Aligned.

Incognito in Relationships

Going incognito does not mean cutting people off. It means cutting off the constant stream of self-abandonment you've normalized to keep the peace. You don't have to disappear from people to disappear for yourself. You can love people deeply and still require distance. You can be committed and still crave solitude. You can care and still go quiet. If someone gets offended because you took time to recalibrate, that's not love.

That's access entitlement. And maybe it's time to stop issuing VIP passes to people who can't handle your boundaries without throwing a fit.

Now, does that mean you never communicate your need for space? Not at all. In relationships worth protecting, clarity is kindness. But clarity isn't the same as permission. You don't need to justify your healing. You don't owe people a play-by-play of your internal process. So instead of over-explaining when people question your retreat, say this: "I'm good, but I'm taking some time for me. I love you. I just need to be quiet for a bit. This isn't about anything between us. It's just something I need to do to reset and take care of myself."

Say it once. Mean it. And move on accordingly. You're not asking for approval. You're honoring your inner compass. Because what's the point of being loved if you can't even breathe in the relationship? What's the point of being seen if it only works when you're performing?

There's a way to go quiet and still stay connected. A way to reset without rupture. A way to disappear without dismantling the love you've built. And that way starts with knowing this: You're not abandoning anyone. You're choosing you.

Silence Without Sabotage

Sometimes the most radical act of love is pulling back because you finally care about *you*. The people closest to you will feel it the most when you shift. When you stop answering every call. When you stop explaining every move. When you stop giving your emotional labor away like samples at a grocery store.

They'll say you're distant. Cold. Different. But maybe different is exactly what you needed to be all along. You don't have to go incognito *against* the people you love. You can go incognito *within* those relationships with boundaries that protect the bond *and* your peace.

Being available 24/7 doesn't prove loyalty; it just proves you don't value your own time and energy. Choosing silence means cutting off the pressure to perform for them. It means not shrinking your needs to keep someone else comfortable. You can love someone deeply and still need distance. You can care and still say, "I'm not in a space to talk right now." You can be present in a relationship and still retreat for your own healing. *You do not need authorization to rest, pause, or protect your peace.* Not even from the people who love you. Especially not from the ones who only love the version of you that gives endlessly and asks for nothing. If they truly love you, they will adjust. If they don't, you've just met the truth you've been avoiding.

Incognito Strategy

This is where the work gets real. If you are going to protect your peace inside relationships, you'll need more than good intentions. You'll need strategies. So let's break this down.

Create sacred silence zones.

Not every moment has to be shared. Choose a time of day or week that is just for you—no check-ins, no calls, no emotional downloads. Let those you care about know, "This is just some time I'm taking to recharge. It's not about anyone else. It's something I need for myself."

Use the gentle close.

Not every moment needs to turn into a deep dive. If a conversation is draining you or hitting at the wrong time, you're allowed to close it without guilt. Try this: "I want to be fully present for this, and I can't be at the moment. Let's pause here." You are protecting your bandwidth. That's grown-woman energy.

Do not overexplain the pause.

You don't have to give people a PowerPoint presentation on your need for space. The truth is, people who respect you won't require a monologue. People who don't will resent you anyway. So save your breath.

Stop giving access.

You don't have to be emotionally accessible just because someone wants you to be. Love does not mean you have to be "on call." Start checking in with yourself before you check in with others. Ask: "Do I have the capacity to hold this right now?" If not, wait. The world will not crumble because you didn't respond immediately.

Practice "quiet love."

Love doesn't always look like talking, texting, or showing up on demand. Sometimes love looks like trusting someone enough to let them be without needing to fix, explain, or update them constantly. Let your silence mean care, not withdrawal.

Build invisible boundaries.

You don't always have to announce a boundary for it to be real. Start shifting your availability without a press release. Decline the call. Don't answer the text right away. Let your absence be your message. People will adjust their expectations to your behavior, not your explanations.

Have one anchor person (optional).

Going incognito doesn't mean isolating entirely. Choose one trusted person who gets it—someone who won't take it personally, who knows you are healing, not hiding. That anchor can be your bridge to the world when you need to step out again.

Incognito at the Family Table

Family will guilt-trip you without even realizing they are doing it. They'll say, "You have changed," when you start protecting your peace. They'll say, "You never call anymore," when you stop answering out of obligation. They'll say, "We're just worried about you," when what they really mean is, "We don't like that we no longer have the same access to you."

You can love your family and still set boundaries so your emotional bandwidth doesn't get hijacked. You don't have to take every call. You don't have to explain your silence. You don't have to attend every family gathering just to prove you care. You protect your relationships by being honest about your limits before the resentment builds.

Try this when you're pulling back: "I love y'all. I'm not pulling away because something is wrong. I just need some time to regroup. Don't take it personally. It's just something I need to do for me." And don't worry if they don't get it. They don't have to. Your peace doesn't require their permission. Going incognito with family does not mean you don't love them. It means you love yourself enough to not be emotionally depleted by them.

Sometimes I disappear not because I am burned out but because I'm locked in. Because I've got something to build. A vision to honor. A chapter that won't write itself. Going incognito is sometimes about the hustle. But not the performative hustle. Not the "Look at me! I'm grinding" kind. This is a quiet grind. A purpose-driven, pressure-tested, power-move energy. There are seasons where the dream requires isolation. Where distractions must die or the vision will. People will take your purpose personally when they no longer have casual access to your time.

REFLECTIONS

Use these to go deeper, disrupt autopilot, and sit with the truth of where you are and who has too much access to you.

1. *Where in your life are you overexposed, and to whom?* Who has front-row access that hasn't earned the seat?

2. *When was the last time you hid on purpose? How did it serve you?* Did it protect your peace, your growth, your healing?

3. *What relationships thrive on your visibility but not your well-being?* Are you on for people who would never show up for you in return?

4. *What does it look like to move in silence during this season?* Describe what "incognito" means for you, not what the world expects.

5. *What role is silence playing in your current growth?* Is it time to speak, or time to disappear for a while and regroup?

TAKEAWAYS

- *Your presence is valuable,* but it's not owed.

- *You don't have to explain your need for space.* Boundaries don't need a PowerPoint presentation.

- *Quiet isn't weakness.* It's wisdom. You don't need to be visible to be powerful. Your progress doesn't require permission.

- *Solitude is strategy.* Disappearing on purpose is how you hear your next instruction.

- *Not everyone deserves the same access to you.* Energy is currency. Spend it where it appreciates in value.

- *Choose a day this week to go incognito.* Log off. Unplug. Tune in. Your highest self is waiting in the silence.

Chapter Twenty Three

The Imbalance Balance

Part of growing to maturity, part of growing up, requires that we recognize and accept that we cannot have it all.
—*Matthew Kelly*

It is impossible to have it all. There will be seasons when you win beyond measure and others when you fail unceremoniously. Balance is like a mythical creature. It's a unicorn of today. When we consider all the facets of life demanding our time and presence, how could balance ever be possible? We all hope to compartmentalize our lives: work in one place, personal life in another. But we must accept that there will be times when the scales are uneven. Balance itself can't bring balance. You must become well-acquainted with imbalance.

To find a semblance of balance, maybe you need to give up your Saturdays to get it together. Or perhaps it's a few hours in the evening you must sacrifice. Balance doesn't come by chance. It doesn't come by comfort either. When I was growing up, I was an obsessive reader, and I've mentioned before how that made all the difference for me. I read at any hour—sometimes until the wee hours of the morning—so much so that when I took my final exam in high school, I achieved the first distinction in English the region had ever earned. Reading was fun for me. But beyond fun, it took effort and time spent at the library almost every school day, making use of new vocabulary. To gain a win, we must give up something. Before we can gain, we will have to give.

What Are You Known For?

Imbalance shows up in your habits. In how people experience you. In what you're known for. Because we're all known for something. Maybe you're known for being reliable, compassionate, and creative. Maybe you're the fixer, the helper, the last-minute miracle-worker. Or maybe you're the one who is always late. Who starts strong and fades. Who overcommits, underdelivers, or ghosts entirely when things get real.

And the people around you? They know. They just might not say it out loud. What are you really known for? And does that align with who you say you want to be? This is where imbalance starts to fester—when what you want to be known for is out of sync with how you show up. You say you want to lead, but you never finish. You say you want peace, but you're always plugged in. You want a better life, but your habits don't support it.

What is one behavior you're known for that needs to go? Not ten. Choose one. Tackle it. Rewire it. Don't just wish for change; become someone new, one habit at a time.

Giving up Comfort

We can usually see when we're drowning in our comfort. If we want change in our life, we have to get uncomfortable. I don't always know how I find time for everything that requires my attention, but I do. I prioritize it. Discomfort should be your friend.

The art of growth lies in investing your time where it will eventually pay off. I wake up at 5:30 every morning. It started as a necessity since my eldest son leaves very early for high school. But now it's a habit. In that quiet time, I read. I start my day before the sun rises, feeding my mind with powerful thoughts. What are you willing to do to make your impact and live your best life? Comfort feels good in the moment, but too much of it, stacked day after day, can quietly crush your dreams. When we think of retirement or "the good life," we should consider which discomforts we'll embrace now in order to enjoy that future.

Can you silence the comforts in your life? Can you turn off the television, exit the gaming app that pulls you in, or close the social media tabs you mindlessly scroll through? Be mindful of your time by first becoming aware. If you want to switch on the good in your life, you have to hit the off switch. Turn your phone on "Do Not Disturb." If your goal is a five-year plan, understand what you're willing to give up. If you're building a meditative, balanced life, excessive partying or overindulging in alcohol are not habits that align with that lifestyle. Giving up comfort should not come at the cost of your sanity, but protecting your sanity may require you to release the comforts that are slowly killing your dreams. And maybe your dream feels like it's on life support right now. You can bring it back to life though.

You own the rights to that vision. And the way you trademark it is by giving up little bits of comfort every single day. It's not glamorous. We'll leave that for social media. In real life—the one you and I live in—there are real problems to solve, real mountains to climb, and legitimate solutions to discover.

My current goal is completing this book. The challenge? Finding the time. Instead of crawling into my cozy bed, I'm sitting at my desk on a Saturday evening, writing these words. I'm giving up time with my kids and my husband right now because the greater good is that I'm creating something much bigger than my life—much bigger than simply watching a movie. I'm showing up for them. They're seeing me fight for this dream in my heart. I'm teaching them how to show up in their lives. They are learning by example how to show up with integrity and accountability. If I can't be accountable to my family, how can I be true to myself? That possibility won't exist if I don't put this goal ahead of other interfering patterns. The same is true for you.

Seesaw Balance

Our lives are like a seesaw. True balance is unattainable. The closest we get is when we're in motion. Sometimes we're up, and sometimes we're down. The downs are where we grow. That's when we uncover truths. The lows force us there—whether we're ready or not. We are pushed into readiness, forced to become better, more resourceful. There is likely going to be pain in the process. But through it, we become more capable of managing our lives and navigating fear.

Life has been busy for me the last couple of years, and I realize it's not slowing down anytime soon. I've wanted to start a local book club, but I danced with the idea for a while until I finally decided it was time to do it. The club's purpose was clear: improve our reading habits, enhance our communication, and build a small network of women. It's been two years since the book club began, and the ladies who stuck around have built tight connections with each other and experienced growth far beyond the club. I can see it clearly. Even though it's a small group, we've spoken up, started new ventures, sharpened our skills in our fields, and had fun along the way.

If you have a dream or goal calling to you, don't worry about what you're giving up now. Your season of wins is coming. If you want to experience those wins, start today.

The Myth of the Scale

We were sold a lie: If we worked hard enough, organized well enough, woke up early enough, then we could have it all—at the same time. Balance doesn't look like a perfectly distributed pie chart. It looks like giving your all in one area while another one sits quietly, waiting its turn. It looks like saying no to a night out because you need to say yes to your future. It's giving up instant gratification so that long-term impact can finally show up and step into the spotlight.

You don't owe balance to the world. You owe commitment to your dream. That means you won't always be caught up in group chats or with the friend who needs a weekly vent session. It means missing bedtime stories sometimes because you're working on building something your children can inherit. It means some days your house will be spotless, and other days your dream will take priority.

The Currency of Change

Change doesn't take coupons. It doesn't respond to half-off sales or clearance racks. If you want change, you're going to have to pay full price—and the currency is you. Time. Focus. Energy. Discipline. That's what it costs.

We live in a world that praises doing the most with the least amount of effort. But real transformation does not work like that. It doesn't ask what's convenient for you. It asks what you're willing to trade. And if you are serious about leveling up, then you must get serious about what you're spending your currency on. Want a better body? The currency is sleep, diet, and sweat. Want to grow a business? The currency is consistency, rejection, and learning while losing. Want deeper relationships? The currency is vulnerability, attention, and time.

Every outcome you crave is sitting behind a payment gate labeled *sacrifice*. We act surprised when things don't change, but we've been stingy with the cost. You want the vision, but you're still paying in pennies of effort. You want legacy, but you're budgeting your focus like you'll get a refund if it doesn't work out. Let me break it to you: There are no refunds in the dream-building process. Only results or regret. Start paying in full.

Ride the Current's Ebb and Flow

In the world of short-term rentals, balance often feels like a myth. The constant turnover, guest communications, and property maintenance can tip the scales, leaving little room for personal time. Yet it's in this imbalance that growth emerges.

Take, for instance, the day I found myself transporting six bags of garbage because the property's bins were overflowing. As I drove home, windows down, I noticed a fly buzzing around. Soon, there were more. The realization hit me: The flies were from the garbage in my car. It was a moment of chaos, yet I couldn't help but laugh. Then there was the time guests dug a massive hole in the yard (who knows why!). Without a shovel, I resorted to using a piece of wood to fill it with rocks. Or the day I learned to restring blinds after someone yanked them too hard. Each challenge was unexpected, each solution improvised.

These experiences taught me that imbalance is merely a catalyst. It's in these moments of discomfort that fortitude is built, skills are honed, and character is forged in fire. You don't control the pull of the ocean's current, but you can learn to ride it with it and flow, finding your rhythm.

The Sacrifice Is the Signal

Choosing to be hands-on in my business was about commitment. While I could delegate tasks, I recognized that being present, especially in the early stages, was crucial. This meant embracing the messiness, the unpredictability, and the exhaustion. Sacrifice became my compass. Every bag of garbage hauled, every makeshift repair, every late-night turnover was a testament to my dedication. These were signals, indicators that I was on the right path, investing in something meaningful.

In the broader landscape of short-term rentals, many hosts face similar challenges. Kerri Gibson, a former tech-industry CPA turned short-term rental entrepreneur, manages six properties under her brand Chalets Hygge. After experiencing corporate burnout in 2017, she pivoted to real estate, starting with a flip in Quebec. She manages six properties and emphasizes that real estate is far from passive income. She dedicates about fifty hours a week to her business, handling everything from turnovers to guest communications, underscoring the hands-on nature of the industry.

Embracing these sacrifices is about recognizing that growth often requires discomfort. It's in these moments that we find clarity, purpose, and the drive to push forward.

REFLECTIONS

1. *Audit your time this week.* Where are your hours going? What comforts are costing you progress?

2. *Name the habit or behavior you are known for that you want to change.* Be honest with yourself. Pick one and focus on it over the next thirty days.

3. *Start a thirty-one-day challenge to reclaim your reputation.* Whether it's punctuality, finishing what you start, or staying consistent—commit and track it daily.

4. *Choose one comfort to cut.* That one thing (social media scrolling, Netflix bingeing, late sleep-ins) is robbing you of your next level. Cut it for the next seven days and journal about the positive changes you experience.

5. *Anchor into your why.* Remind yourself what the sacrifice is for. Write it out. Tape it somewhere you can see when you feel tempted to slip.

6. *Take imperfect action.* Don't wait for a perfect window of time. Steal a moment. Trade an evening. Use a Saturday. Just move.

TAKEAWAYS

- *You cannot have it all, and that's okay.* Trying to keep everything in balance at all times is a myth. Trade-offs are necessary.

- *Balance does not come by chance or comfort.* It takes intentional decisions, sacrifices, and daily recommitments.

- *Discomfort is not your enemy.* It is your growth partner. Embrace the moments that push you, stretch you, and require more from you.

- *You are known for something.* Make sure it's what you want to be known for. Your habits shape how the world experiences you.

- *Seasons of imbalance often create the biggest wins.* Don't fear the seesaw. Use it.

Chapter Twenty Four

Silent Investors

Refusing to ask for help when you need it is refusing someone the chance to be helpful.

—Lorena Poppe

Your life isn't a solo climb. Your biggest dreams are not waiting at the top of some mountain you scale alone, breathless, bloody, and broken, just so you can say, "I did it myself." That's your ego talking. Not your true and lasting impact.

Legacy-driven growth is communal. It's relational. It's spiritual. You need people. Not just warm bodies on the sideline. You need silent investors who pour into you when the spotlight isn't on, when no one is clapping, when you're hanging on by a thread.

Rewrite the Superwoman Narrative

The world worships the woman who "does it all." But there is no trophy for doing it all while quietly dying inside. We've been force-fed this Superwoman archetype—flawless, unbothered, high-achieving, and somehow still baking homemade muffins at seven a.m. That woman? She's a marketing fantasy. Let her go. Doing it all isn't the flex. Doing what matters—and letting your people help—is the real power move.

As strong as my mom is, she has always led her life leaning on her tribe. When I was growing up, that tribe was her sisters. At any moment, she could leave my brother and me in their care if she needed to—no questions asked. When I was born, my mom's youngest sister, Aunty Guy (aka my second mom) lived with us. She helped raise my brother and me, and her role in our lives was pivotal, especially during those early first years. Excuses were never given. It was simply understood that my aunts would show up for each other. That was the example I was raised with. And I'm proud to say they stood in the gap when Mom needed them most.

My Real Investors

In my home, the silent investors wear sneakers and hoodies. My eldest son doesn't need a gold star as a reward for sweeping the kitchen or caring for his bird. He does it because he has been trusted. Empowered. Spoken into. The investment is not in what he does; it is in who he is becoming.

My youngest? One ask is all it takes. That's it. No lecture. No meltdown. Just, "Okay, Mama." That's legacy in motion. And my husband? We run a silent partnership like a well-oiled machine. No nagging. No keeping score. If I need him, he moves. If he needs me, I show up. We operate from mutual respect, not martyrdom. That's what silent investment looks like: quiet but consistent.

Pride Is a Dream Killer

Let's talk about the pride problem. Not the kind that keeps your chin up, but the kind that keeps your hand down when you need to raise it and ask for help. Pride whispers, *No one will do it like you.* But they don't need to. Perfection is not the point. Progress is. Legacy is. Freedom is. If you're still trying to micromanage every detail, thinking that's how you maintain control, you are building a prison. One brick of resentment at a time. Let it go.

To finish this manuscript, I had to disappear. Not in a glamorous spa-day, mimosa-on-the-patio kind of way. No. I packed up my laptop and a weekend bag, left the house, and found a quiet place just for me. I needed silence, space, and permission to be unavailable. I spent five hours at a time holed up in the library or camped out in Starbucks and came back to the rental with my mind on fire and my body bone tired.

But I didn't do it alone. Before I left, I woke up early and cooked for three hours—meals for the boys, meals for my husband, meals to hold the house together while I focused on holding myself together. My husband took over the kitchen the next day. My sons stepped up with chores and the little things that make a house move smoothly. I asked for help, and they gave it—without hesitation.

Pride would have told me to push through. Pride would have told me to write the final chapters between loads of laundry, Kumon lessons, and taekwondo practice. Pride would have told me to wait until everything else was done. But dreams don't wait for perfect conditions. They respond to movement. Mine needed me to move out of the house, out of the excuses, and out of the mindset that I had to do it all alone. Sometimes, the greatest thing you can do for your dream is to sit your pride down and walk out the door anyway.

The Real Return on Delegation

You know what else pride hides? Growth. Not just yours but theirs. When you hold everything, you exhaust yourself and rob the people around you of their chance to stretch. Think of the single mom who finally asks her preteen to wash and fold his laundry. At first, it's a heavy load both literally and metaphorically. Maybe the clothes are washed on the wrong cycle or the colors get bleached. But by week three, that kid starts owning it. Or the wife who always managed the bills because she thought her husband wouldn't do it "right." But once she handed over the login info and the trust, she saw him rise with pride in his eyes because he was finally given space to lead.

Delegation isn't dumping. It's design. It's strategic. It's dignified. It says, "I believe in you enough to let you carry this." Let your kids pack their own lunches. Let your spouse plan the weekend. Let your team fumble through the first draft. And when they ask, "Did I do it right?" remind them (and yourself) that anything done with heart wins over anything done with resentment.

Delegation Is a Discipline

Delegation is a leadership move that says, "I trust you. We rise together. This isn't just my dream; it's our legacy." Let your kids carry their weight. Let your spouse carry the vision with you. Let your team take the baton and run. And if they fumble? Let them learn. The muscle of support is only built through use.

Delegation takes humility. It requires loosening your grip, silencing the voice that says, "I'll just do it myself because it'll be faster and better." That mindset may serve you in the short term, but it will burn you out in the long run. Real leadership means teaching others how to rise— not just rising alone.

When I first started delegating in my business, I struggled. I wanted things done a certain way, on a certain timeline, with a certain level of polish. But over time, I realized that holding on too tightly was actually stifling the very growth I was praying for. Once I allowed others to step in—whether it was hiring help, involving my family, or outsourcing tasks that didn't need me—everything shifted. Things didn't always go perfectly, but the freedom it gave me was worth every bump along the way.

The same is true at home. When you teach your kids how to pack their lunches, clean their rooms, or contribute to dinner prep, you're equipping them for life. You're instilling capability, confidence, and character. You're raising contributors, not spectators.

Delegation is less about perfection and more about preparation. It prepares your family to function without constant hand-holding. It prepares your business to operate without burnout. And most importantly, it prepares you to lead from a place of trust instead of control.

So start small. Hand off one task this week that you normally clutch with white knuckles. Let someone else take the wheel—whether it's a spreadsheet, a school drop-off, or a creative decision you usually make. Will it feel scary? Probably. Will it be perfect? Probably not. But it will be powerful. Because when you stop doing everything, you create space for everyone to rise.

Affirmation as a Team Act

You want to crown yourself daily? Beautiful. Do it. Speak it. But know this: Affirmations don't work in isolation. They take root when you are surrounded by people who believe them with you.

Every time I speak mine aloud, I feel the echo of my household catching them in the air. That energy? That's a house built on faith. On effort. On trust. Affirm what you are and let your people echo it back. Affirmations aren't just for you; they're for your circle too.

When I speak life into myself each morning, I'm charging my day *and* charging my family. They hear me say, "I am an author." They hear me declare, "I am building something powerful." That energy sticks. My boys have started speaking their own. I've heard them tell each other, "You got this," and say things like, "I'm good at that" without flinching. This is generational wealth. Not just in dollars but in confidence, in belief, in knowing who they are and what they can become.

Speak life so loudly into your own soul that your people catch the echo. Say it so often that your home starts believing it with you. Let your affirmations become a chorus—because when a household believes, it builds something unshakable.

The Emotional Currency of Support

Support is emotional currency. Every task taken off your plate is a vote for your peace. Every errand handled is an investment in your clarity. Every dinner made by someone else is a deposit in your purpose.

Your team (family, friends, coworkers) does not need to be perfect. They need to be activated. Empowered. And that starts with you releasing the reins. The hardest part of letting go is watching them do it differently. It's watching your daughter fold the towels in the "wrong" way. It's seeing your husband load the dishwasher like it's a game of Tetris gone wrong. It's your assistant missing the tone of an email or your friend dropping the ball on a favor. But you know what? They're still doing it. And that counts. When you micromanage everything, you become the bottleneck. You become the reason the dream slows down. Because everything must filter through you.

Let the towels be wonky. Let the emails be sent. Let them fumble and figure it out. Because as they grow, you grow. And suddenly, you have a team, not just a to-do list. You have co-builders, not just spectators. And in the moments where it all clicks (the groceries are stocked, the laundry is folded, your writing flows, and your purpose feels held), you realize it wasn't about getting help. It was about building a life where everyone has a hand in the masterpiece.

REFLECTIONS

1. Identify your silent investors. Write a thank-you note. Speak it. Text it. Make it real.

2. Choose three tasks to delegate this week. Track the emotional lift, not just the time saved.

3. Find a support group, tribe, or accountability partner. Real connection fuels real goals.

4. Speak your affirmations daily, but this time include one about receiving help.

5. Let someone help you this week, and resist the urge to "fix" how they do it. Let their way be enough.

TAKEAWAYS

- Your mission is too big for a party of one.

- Support is strategy, not a surrender.

- Delegation is discipline, not deficiency.

- Pride might look powerful, but it will bankrupt your dreams.

- Speak your vision, and build a team that believes it too.

Chapter Twenty Five

Identity Idiosyncrasy

Unlike a drop of water which loses its identity when it joins the ocean, man does not lose his being in the society in which he lives. Man's life is independent. He is born not for the development of the society alone, but for the development of his self.
—B.R. Ambedkar

There is only one you. One mind, one body, one soul stitched together with the quirks, bruises, brilliance, contradictions, and identity idiosyncrasies that make you, *you.*

According to Merriam-Webster, *identity* is the "distinguishing character or personality of an individual." That's cute. But we know better. Your identity isn't just a label or a bullet point on a resume. It's the unseen fire behind your eyes. The way you move through a room, the rhythm in your walk, the sharpness in your silence, or the melody in your laugh. It's the collection of oddities you've been told to tone down, your stubbornness, your sarcasm, your softness, your steel. These are your identity idiosyncrasies, and they're not flaws. They're fingerprints.

Identity is personal. Sacred. Inherited. Earned. Even in a sea of people, you stand apart. I see it in my boys, who were raised under the same roof, fed from the same table, loved by the same hands. Yet they couldn't be more different. My firstborn is all presence. Confident. Certain. He takes his time with things, especially food. It's like he is too busy analyzing the universe to bother with chewing. My little one, on the other hand, is fire and appetite. Disciplined. Resourceful. Lives fully in the moment and never misses a meal. Same home. Same love. Different blueprints. That's identity. That's the invisible DNA of the soul.

No matter how closely you align with someone—whether you've mirrored their walk, their hustle, or their vibe—you will never be them. And they will never be you. You can admire someone, learn from them, and even echo pieces of them for a time, but eventually, the real you will always surface. And she is not meant to be a copy. She is the original. She is the prototype.

Your weird is the good stuff! The way you speak with your hands, or the fact that you fold laundry in your head while smiling at someone's story—that's you. The subtle nose swipe when you are deep in thought, the way your voice rises a half-octave when you are passionate. Those little things matter. They make you memorable.

So what if you're not the loudest in the room? Or the funniest? Or the trendiest? Maybe you are the one who observes first. Maybe you're the one who doesn't speak unless it's meaningful. Maybe you're the one who slips out early from the party and leaves behind a lingering impression. Good. Leave your imprint. Not everyone has to be the fireworks. Some of us are the embers that last long after the show.

Dualities of the Self

I'm writing this chapter from a plane heading to Miami. I looked out the window earlier and saw something that shook me—a split in the ocean. To my left, emerald-green waters. To my right, a deep, endless blue. One body, two colors. Two truths in one space.

Isn't that us? We are contradictions. Living, breathing paradoxes. We are tender and tough. Bold and unsure. Secure in one moment and unraveling the next. And that's okay. It's exactly where your identity idiosyncrasies live—in the spaces where your duality dares to coexist.

You are not weak because you doubt yourself sometimes. You are not abnormal because you need solitude or because you crave connection. You are not too much because your energy fills a room. Nor are you too little if you find joy in the shadows. You are exactly as you should be—unfinished, evolving, complex, and complete all at once.

We are walking, breathing identity idiosyncrasies—half shadow, half light. Half certainty, half what-the-hell-am-I-doing? And if that makes you feel a little unhinged sometimes, then good. That means you are alive. You have been taught to pick one lane—strong or soft, loud or quiet, this or that. But you can be more than one thing. You already are. And the sooner you stop apologizing for the contradictions, the freer you'll feel.

Sometimes defining your identity requires a reinvention. When you become a mother. When you leave a job. When your name changes. When your dreams shift. You're becoming someone new. And that version deserves just as much love as the last one. So don't chase a version of yourself that exists only on a pedestal. Love the you who wakes up unsure. Love the you who procrastinates, then crushes the deadline. Love the you who forgets, forgives, flares up, folds laundry at two a.m., writes poetry on the back of receipts, overthinks, over-loves, and still shows up. There is no formula. There is only you. All of you. And every inch of that is worthy.

The Mic Still Worked

I remember when I first started public speaking. My palms would sweat, and my heart would beat so loud I swore the audience could hear it too. I used to believe I had to be overprepared—every word written out, rehearsed, revised, timed to perfection. I thought mastery came from knowing every single line. But over time, I learned something else entirely. I learned that the mic still worked, even when I didn't know exactly what I was going to say. The power wasn't in the script. The power was in the presence. It was in me. The confidence came because I finally trusted myself to show up and let who I was speak— flaws, pauses, stumbles, and all. And what's wild is that during those unscripted moments is when the room leaned in. When people felt something real.

That's what identity is. It's not about memorizing a version of who we think we should be. It's not even about performing that version for applause. Identity is about trusting that who you are in this moment—with all your identity idiosyncrasies on display— is enough. That you can stand at the front of the room, the edge of a chapter, the precipice of a decision—and even if you don't have it all figured out, you still have something to say. Your mic still works.

We are so conditioned to wait until we've got the "right" story to tell, the polished version of ourselves to present. But sometimes the magic happens when we speak before we're fully ready. When we walk into a room carrying nothing but the weight of our lived experience and the courage to be seen anyway. That's where identity speaks loudest—when it's unrehearsed, unfiltered, and undeniably yours.

REFLECTIONS

A Permission Slip to Be You

Tear this out. Screenshot it. Tattoo it on your soul.

I, [insert your name here], give myself full permission to:

Be both calm and chaotic.

Be quiet in loud rooms and loud in quiet ones.

Feel unsure but still show up.

Take breaks without guilt.

Own my presence without apology.

Be soft, even when the world demands hardness.

Say "I don't know" and not feel lesser.

Evolve, backslide, re-emerge, and repeat.

Redefine who I am as many times as I damn well need.

Wear the red lipstick one day and skip makeup the next.

Laugh loudly. Cry freely. Cuss occasionally. Pray often.

Not fit into someone else's idea of what I should be.

Love all my quirks, dualities, identity idiosyncrasies, and fire.

Be fully me—unpolished, in-process, and still powerful.

Signed: Me. (In real ink.)

Date: [The day I chose wholeness over perfection.]

Checklist For The Real You

(when the world tries to edit your identity)

☐ Did I try to shrink myself to fit into a space today?

☐ Did I compare my personality to someone else's highlight reel?

☐ Did I feel guilty for needing time alone or time with people?

☐ Did I hide something I love because it felt "too different"?

☐ Did I celebrate a weird quirk or gift that makes me, me?

☐ Did I honor my energy, whether that meant saying yes or no?

☐ Did I choose authenticity over approval, even once today?

If you answered yes to any of these, then darling, you're doing just fine.

TAKEAWAYS

- *You are not here to blend in.* The things that make you different were never mistakes. They were divinely planted quirks, ticks, tones, and textures that set your frequency apart. Stop apologizing for them.

- *Duality is your birthright.* You can be soft and strong, uncertain and powerful, reserved and radiant. Don't shrink yourself to fit one mold. You are not a single story. You are a full anthology.

- *Comparison is a thief, and identity is your armor.* Trying to imitate someone else's glow only dims your own. Embrace the parts of you that feel too weird, too loud, too much—they are likely your most magnetic features.

- *You don't have to explain your becoming.* Your growth will confuse the version of you people were most comfortable with. That is not your burden to carry. Transform anyway.

- *Love yourself now, not just later.* Don't wait until you're polished or successful or validated. Start showing love to the version of you that is figuring it out in real time. She deserves that grace.

- *Your uniqueness is an offering.* The way you move through the world—the pauses, the mannerisms, the preferences, the identity idiosyncrasies—are all part of your message. Let people experience you, unfiltered.

- *You are the blueprint.* There is no one you have to become first. No template to follow. Everything you are (right now) is enough to start building something extraordinary.

- *Your identity is your mountain.* It may shift, erode, grow, or quake—but it is yours. Rise from it. Speak from it. Stand on it.

Chapter Twenty Six

Thoughtful Retrospection

Sometimes you have to look back, not to regret, but to remember who you were before the world told you who to be.

—Unknown

The foundation of your past—the choices you've made, the silences you've kept, the words you wished you hadn't said—have all materialized into your now. This is your life. This is the terrain you're walking. And no, it's not always fair. But it is yours. And what you do with it from here? That's where power starts.

We talk about life like it's a puzzle, but what if it's more like a map? Not a detailed folded map you get from the visitor center, but one of those ancient, burned-at-the-corners kind, drawn in pencil and dotted with sweat, full of detours, crossed-out plans, and that one route you swore you'd never take again but did. That's the map of becoming. It's about learning how to read the signs. Recognizing the forks. Naming the traps. And seeing the moment you stopped surviving and started navigating.

Retrospection is how you learn to read your map. Thoughtful retrospection is how you stop getting lost in your own life. We often think confidence is found by looking forward through goal-setting, vision-boarding, hustle-and-proving. But real confidence? The kind that doesn't tremble when people misunderstand you or misname you? That kind is rooted in retrospection. In your willingness to go back, face the echoes, and distinguish them from your current voice. Confidence is clarity. It's choosing to tell the truth about who you are, even if no one claps for it.

Echoes from the Past

We are walking archives. We carry the voices of teachers who called us "gifted" and of coaches who said we weren't trying hard enough. We carry praise and pain in equal measure. And without retrospection, we let echoes dictate our decisions.

I still remember one of mine. I was in elementary school. Every morning, before she even spoke a word, we'd hear the sharp *click-clack* of her heels echoing down the hallway like a warning bell. She always carried her weapon of choice: a long, thin cane whip. Corporal punishment was still allowed then—and she wielded it with precision. Fear didn't creep in. It slammed into me. The moment she stepped into the room, my body would tense. My palms would sweat. My stomach would twist in knots. I tried to shrink myself, hoping I'd be invisible that day.

But when she stood at the front of the room to teach math—I couldn't follow. My brain would shut down. My ears would buzz. Nothing made sense, no matter how hard I tried. If I got something wrong? The cane would slice through the air and land on bare skin. The pain was sharp, stinging, immediate—followed by raised red welts that burned long after the classroom fell silent. Those marks didn't just live on my skin. They etched themselves into my memory. Over time, math became a symbol of fear. Confusion. Powerlessness. And even years later, I didn't realize that my "dislike of math" wasn't about numbers—

it was about the echo of that classroom. The echo of not feeling safe enough to learn.

You hear that voice when you sit still for too long. That one that says, "You're lazy." Or the one that says, "Don't speak up or you'll sound stupid." Maybe you've heard that you always mess things up at the end, or you're too much. Those are echoes.

But then there's your present voice. That gut-deep truth that whispers, *I'm not who I was. I'm wiser. I'm softer, but I'm sharper.* That voice doesn't scream, but it stands firm. It doesn't have to defend itself. It simply knows. The work of retrospection is about learning which voice is which. Learning that not every thought deserves a seat at your table. That not every internal sound is truth. Some of it is leftover noise. Outdated software. Stories that expired three versions ago.

Posture Is a Language

The world hears us before we open our mouths. Our posture is a paragraph. Our eye contact, a paragraph more. When I was younger, I used to slouch everywhere I went because my spirit hurt, not my back. I didn't realize it then, but my body was echoing the lie that said I didn't belong.

That I should shrink to be more likable or more forgettable.

It took me years to realize that standing tall is like engaging in spiritual warfare. That every straightened spine is a rebellion against erasure. That good posture is about being present. And present you? She's not hiding anymore.

Grace Under Fire

I have a friend, let's call her Grace. She went through a divorce after twenty years of marriage. A long chapter, rewritten. Her split was a full-life detour. She had to move. Rebuild. Start a new career and reimagine what was next. I know it cost her. I know she probably broke down in ways no one ever saw. But on the outside? Grace. Poise. Head held high. Not because she felt strong every day, but because she chose dignity as her default. And that choice shaped her.

Her confidence was forged not in the absence of pain but in the presence of it. That's the truth we don't talk about enough. Confidence is the decision to walk through hardship without letting it strip your name. She didn't let the echoes win. She let them teach her but not lead her. She let the past speak, but not speak for her. That's confidence. Not being bulletproof but being fully you—with the bullet holes, with the questions, with the rebuilds—still standing.

What You Rehearse You Remember

Too many of us spend our energy rehearsing what others said, what they did, or what went wrong. We replay these old scenes instead of examining our own intentions. We become curators of someone else's script. But confidence grows when you start rehearsing your voice. When you stop rewatching what broke you and start listening to what rebuilt you. When you walk into a new season, are you guided by echoes or by clarity? Are you making choices from healed insight or old pain? Are you performing safety or living truth?

Know-Ability over Likability

We've confused knowing ourselves with making ourselves likable. But those two are not twins; they're barely cousins. "Know-ability" is your anchor. When you know who you are, you don't entertain confusion as a hobby. You don't ask people for their blueprint if they've never even built anything real. You stop outsourcing your worth to people who wouldn't recognize your brilliance even if you spelled it out in neon. Know-ability means you know when to stay, when to walk away, and when to pause without panic. It's the muscle memory of having your own back. It's being fluent in your own voice.

So yes, look back. Not to be stuck, but to be sharp. To understand the map you've been drawing in real time. To notice the places you skipped, the ones you stayed too long in, and the surprising turns that led you somewhere better than you planned.

This is the thoughtful retrospection that builds confidence. Not performance. Not applause. Just knowing who you are, how you got here, and why you won't go back to who you had to be to survive. Because now, you are becoming. And the path forward has your name on it.

Confidence in Being You

The past is a compass. But only if you're brave enough to turn around and read it. Some people say you shouldn't look back. That retrospection keeps you stuck, traps you in what was. But let's get something clear: There is a difference between getting stuck in the past and actually learning from it. Between looping old scenes and finally hearing what those old scenes were trying to say.

You want confidence? Start with self-truth. Start with being willing to walk into your mirror room, shut the door behind you, and really look. Not just at who you are today, but at who you were when you cracked, when you stumbled, when you soared. That full reflection—edges, bruises, glows, scars—is what gives you authority to stand tall now.

No Lies Allowed in the Mirror Room

There is a place in your mind where only your unfiltered self exists. No front. No makeup. No curated posts. Just you in full truth. This is the mirror room, where you have to go when you want clarity. When you want to know why you act the way you do, why certain people can rattle your peace, or why that one sentence from ten years ago still stings. It's where you stand eye to eye with your past choices and don't flinch.

Some of us avoid the mirror room like it's on fire. What if we don't like what we see? What if the version of us from three years ago embarrasses the hell out of us today? That's the point. That discomfort is your growth trying to catch up to your body. If you are still living by the echo of something someone said to you when you were seventeen, or by the rhythm of fear from your last big failure or experience, you are giving your past too much power.

Mirror Moments from My Childhood

I was there when it happened. I was just a child, at home with my mother, when a man who owed her money stormed up our steps in broad daylight. I remember the thud of his footsteps, the tension in the air before anything was said. And then, out of nowhere, he punched my mother in the face.

Everything slowed down. The noise. The fear. My breath. I remember the shock—frozen in place, not fully able to process what I'd just witnessed. I couldn't understand how someone could be so violent, so bold, so shameless. It was one of the most traumatic moments of my childhood, and I carried it like a silent weight for a long time.

But what happened next? That became my mirror. My mother didn't crumble. She didn't let fear silence her or shame make her small. She took him to court. She stood tall. She pressed charges and showed up—day after day—accompanied by my aunt, who stood beside her in quiet strength. And she won.

That experience rewired something in me. I saw with my own eyes what it meant to fight back—not with fists but with dignity. To turn pain into power. My mother could have hidden. She could have taken the hit, both physically and metaphorically, and let it go. But she didn't. She chose justice. She chose herself. And that choice echoes in me to this day.

When I walk into the mirror room now—the space where I face my fears, my patterns, my old wounds—I don't just see my own reflection. I see my mother's strength reflected in me. I see someone who was hurt but not broken. Who stood in court instead of staying home in silence. Who taught me, not through words, but through her own brave becoming that we do not have to live inside what someone else tried to do to us.

Your Past Is Not a Life Sentence

Every step you've taken has left you clues. But most people don't stop long enough to trace the path. They just react, move, repeat. But I challenge you to zoom out and ask:

- Why do I keep choosing this kind of relationship?

- Why do I keep over-explaining myself when I say no?

- Where did that narrative originate?

When you step back, you will begin to see your internal code. The one you didn't even know was running in the background. This is where know-ability becomes your weapon. When you know yourself, you stop being confused by your own reactions. You stop letting other people's voices sound louder than your own. You don't need algorithm-driven advice, surface-level quotes, or recycled opinions. You are the source.

Confidence is not born from praise; it's born from understanding. You've got to be willing to be your own narrator. Not just the main character but the one telling the story. You have spent enough years being narrated by others. The version of you shaped by trauma. The one filtered by your mother's guilt, your father's expectations, your ex's rejection. You've listened to enough echoes. Now it's time to speak in your voice.

Most of our reflection doesn't happen in silence; it happens in interaction. The mirror reflects the truth in the way your child looks at you after a harsh word. It's carved out in the silence between texts. It's chiseled into every conflict, every reconnection, every time you overextend or finally say no. Relationships are mirrors. Some are clear, some are distorted, some are shattered—but every single one is reflective.

If you really want to know who you are, study who you've been in relation to others. Not from a place of blame or self-shame but from raw honesty. When did you abandon your voice to keep the peace? When did you raise your voice because silence felt too vulnerable? When did you contort yourself into a version of you that made someone else comfortable?

This is about decoding the past so you can decide what parts of your relational behavior were survival and what parts were truth. There's a difference between who you were in the room and who you really are. Relational reflection invites you to stop pretending that other people didn't shape you. That heartbreak didn't restructure your trust. That friendship didn't rewire your hope. That conversation didn't reframe how you view yourself. All of it matters.

That's the power of thoughtful retrospection. You stop gaslighting your own experience. You stop minimizing the impact. You start seeing how the people who entered your story—even the wrong ones—helped you excavate the right parts of yourself.

REFLECTIONS

Your Mirror Room Check-In

1. What is one moment from your past that still echoes in your decision-making today?

_____

_____

2. Who was I trying to protect or impress with that decision I regret?

_____

_____

3. What did my younger self need to hear that I can give her now?

_____

_____

4. What are three repeated patterns in my life—and what are they trying to teach me?

_____

_____

5. How do I want to sound when I speak to myself in five years?

_____

_____

TAKEAWAYS

• *Confidence isn't loud, but it is clear.* Clarity comes from knowing where you've been and what it's made you.

• *Grace is power under control.* You can crumble on the inside and still stand like a force on the outside.

• *Be your own narrator.* If you let someone else hold the mic to your life, don't be surprised if they misquote you.

• *Revisit your past not to relive it, but to release it.* Don't carry echoes into rooms they were never meant to fill.

Chapter Twenty Seven

Possibility Mindset

The future belongs to those who believe in the beauty of their dreams.

—Eleanor Roosevelt

What's possible for you? Have you ever truly asked yourself that question from wild, childlike wonder? As children, we live in pure possibility. We dream audaciously: to be astronauts, scientists, entrepreneurs, changemakers. We are fearless in our belief that we can be anything.

Adulthood undoubtedly drapes itself in detours: debt, obligations, loss, exhaustion, heartbreak. The dreams that once danced so clearly in our minds become faint echoes.

As a child, You didn't overthink it. You didn't calculate the cost. There were no ceilings, only sky.

Somewhere along the way, though, many of us lose that possibility mindset. We tuck away our dreams for safekeeping, but too often we forget where we put them. Life steps in with its never-ending demands—bills, caretaking, job stress, family obligations. And possibility begins to feel like a luxury we can't afford.

Possibility isn't gone. It's waiting for you to pick it back up again. I know because I've lived it. Writing this book didn't come easy. I started two years ago, full of energy and a big vision. And then life got in the way. I stopped at 7,000 words. It wasn't until I reconnected with my why—my desire to help others, to offer something meaningful to the world—that I picked up my pen again. That fire came back. I remembered that this book was a bridge to the impact I wanted to make. That's what possibility looks like; it's the intersection of purpose and belief, no matter how messy the middle is.

Reset Mindset

Sometimes, you must begin again. After my father passed, my mother had every reason to fold. Grief hit hard. Confusion loomed. She was raising two kids, and her world had been turned upside down. But she didn't crumble—not in front of us. She stood tall and carried the weight of our dreams on her shoulders. She chose hope even when it didn't feel real. Because of her, we knew how to find the light when it felt like the sun had disappeared.

She didn't pretend life was perfect. But even in her most broken moments, she made the quiet decision to hold on to the possibility that healing was still ahead, that her story could still shift, that life had more waiting for her than what she was currently experiencing. That belief got passed down to me. I carry it in everything I do. And now, I'm passing it on to you.

There will be moments when you're stuck, tired, lost. You might forget what you're capable of. That's when you borrow hope. From a friend. From a mentor. From a book. From your own past where you overcame the last hard thing. Because you did overcome it, and you will again.

Relighting the Flame

What does possibility look like now for you? It's no longer the childhood fantasy. It's not about castles in the sky. Now it's grittier. More grounded. It's waking up early to write, taking a course when your schedule is full, healing from heartbreak and choosing to love again, standing up for yourself when it's uncomfortable. Possibility now means choice. Power. Intention. Possibility means redefining your story even when it feels like life already wrote the ending for you. You are not too late. It is not too hard. And you are not too broken. If you're breathing, there is still more for you.

Suspend Disbelief

Before anything shifts in your world, it has to shift in your mind. This is the sacred space where change begins— where the unseen becomes possible, and the improbable becomes personal. This is where you learn to suspend disbelief.

You have done this before, whether you realize it or not. Every time you've watched a movie and let yourself get pulled into the world of magic, or time travel, or intergalactic battles, you've suspended disbelief. You've willingly let go of logic to immerse yourself in a story that stirred something inside you. That same mindset (the one you activate at the movies) is the one you need in real life when you choose to believe in your own transformation before it has proof.

When I picked up my pen again after stopping, I had no guarantee that the words would flow or that anyone would care. But I suspended disbelief. I imagined what could happen if I kept going. I remembered that the reason I started was bigger than me. I knew this book could help someone else find themselves again. I chose to believe in that impact, even when doubt tried to make itself comfortable in the corners of my mind.

Suspending disbelief means you trust that your current reality isn't the full story. It means you choose vision over fear and faith over facts. It means you say yes to your future self, even while your present self is still figuring it out.

The most powerful people I know aren't the ones who had everything figured out; they are the ones who moved anyway. They believed in a version of themselves they hadn't met yet. And so they kept showing up. They kept trying. They kept building. Can you suspend disbelief long enough to see what is possible for you? Can you keep believing even when the results don't show up right away? Can you act like your dream is real, because it is?

The Art of Suspending Disbelief

When it comes to suspending disbelief, it's more than just a mental trick; it's about practicing a radical shift in perception. This means seeing beyond the obvious, the current limitations, and choosing to entertain possibility over certainty. Often, our world can feel very fixed. Our circumstances, routines, and even our self-image can make us feel like the future has already been written. The most powerful way to break out of this is to interrupt that fixed thinking with the audacious act of believing in the unrealized.

It is an act of intentional surrender. It's what allows us to fully enter a story, an idea, or an experience that might not seem logical or provable but still feels true in a deeper way. It's the quiet agreement we make with a book, a film, a dream, or even a possibility: *I know this may not make sense, but I'm going to let it in anyway.*

Suspending disbelief is an invitation to move beyond the rigid mind that demands evidence, control, and certainty and instead access the part that thrives on wonder, imagination, and intuition. It's the shift from thinking, *This can't be real* to, *What if it is?*

The Mental Shift

Suspending disbelief means creating space between what you see in front of you and what you believe can happen. It's a conscious choice to stop defining your future by your present circumstances and tap into the power of vision.

When you do this, you allow yourself to reframe the stories you tell yourself.

You've probably told yourself stories of limitations: "I'm too old to start this," or "I don't have enough experience," or "It's too late." These stories often become the barrier between you and your next step. In order to suspend disbelief, start by asking: "What if those beliefs are just stories? What if they aren't the truth but merely a past narrative holding you back?"

Trusting the Unseen

Suspending disbelief is powerful because you don't need to see the path completely laid out before you to take the first step. Just like a seed buried underground, you may not see the progress or the result of your effort right away. But just because you can't see it doesn't mean it's not happening.

Suspending disbelief is also about trusting that growth is happening beneath the surface. It's the same process as when you start a fitness routine. You don't see the physical change right away, but your body is transforming nonetheless. Likewise, your dreams are transforming too—albeit in unseen ways. And that's where the magic happens: in the faith you have when you can't yet see the fruits of your labor.

Belief in Yourself

What often holds us back from this radical belief is not the lack of possibility but the fear of being let down. What if I try and fail? What if the belief is misplaced? It's natural to feel fear, but it's essential to understand that fear often comes from a lack of self-trust. Believing in yourself means that regardless of the outcome, you are committed to showing up anyway.

What would it look like if you could fully suspend disbelief and believe that your future self is already on the other side of your current struggles? What might change if you acted as though anything were possible for you right now?

REFLECTIONS

1. *Reflect on Your Limitations*: Write about a time when you believed something was impossible for you. What beliefs were holding you back? What was the outcome when you decided to challenge those beliefs (even if only in thought)? What did you learn from that experience?

2. *Describe Your Dream Self*: Imagine that you've fully suspended disbelief and you're living your dream life. What does that look like? How do you feel in your body, your mind, and your emotions? Write a letter to yourself from that version of you. What advice would your future self give you right now?

3. *What Are the Stories You Tell Yourself*? What limiting beliefs do you carry about your abilities? How might you start to change the narrative in your mind? Write a counter-story to one of your most ingrained beliefs. If you've always thought, *I can't do X*, write a new belief that says, "I can . . ."

4. *Take Action Despite Fear*: Write down one area of your life where you are currently afraid to take the first step. What would you do if you suspended disbelief and acted like you had nothing to lose? What small step can you take today to move forward?

TAKEAWAYS

● *Your mind is a gateway to new possibilities.* Remember, your mindset is the starting point of all transformation. By choosing to suspend disbelief and believing in what hasn't happened yet, you open the door to all sorts of opportunities. What is possible for you starts with your willingness to imagine it.

● *Growth happens in the unseen.* Even when you can't see immediate results, trust that growth is happening beneath the surface. Don't expect overnight success. Embrace the journey and trust the process, even when the path is unclear.

● *Your power is in your actions.* Belief alone isn't enough. Action is the bridge between where you are and where you want to be. The belief in possibility must be paired with daily intentional steps, even when they feel small or insignificant. You can't create transformation from a place of stagnation.

● *Suspend disbelief, and create your future.* Practice suspending disbelief in all areas of your life. When you step into a space of possibility, you allow yourself to create a future that once seemed impossible. Don't let doubt stop you. Use it as fuel to keep believing in what you can achieve.

Chapter Twenty Eight

Internal Validation

When we consistently suppress and distrust our intuitive knowingness, looking instead for authority, validation, and approval from others, we give our personal power away.

—Shakti Gawain

Who are you when no one is clapping? This single question has the power to crack the foundation of who we think we are. Because in a world that thrives on applause, on likes, on performance reviews, and on digital praise, we must pause and ask: What remains when the noise stops?

According to the Cambridge Dictionary, *validation* is "the feeling that other people approve of or accept you." And we are living in a time where that definition is currency. So many of us, knowingly or not, have turned our lives into a performance, hoping to gain the recognition, love, or applause that makes us feel *worthy*. But external validation, though temporarily gratifying, is unstable ground. It can lift you one moment and abandon you the next.

We hustle for it. We overextend ourselves, strive for impossible goals, earn degrees, promotions, applause, love. But all of that will never be enough if we don't first validate ourselves. Because all the recognition in the world won't sustain a soul that feels unseen by its own owner.

Let's break this down. Why do we crave validation? Because we want to feel valid. We want to know we matter, that we're loved, that we belong. But if the answer to our worth is always outside of us, we are forever at the mercy of other people's moods, projections, and opinions. That's a losing game. What if the only approval we needed was our own?

Validity

Let me say this clearly: I am not talking about staying silent in the face of injustice. If you are being mistreated or unfairly passed over at work, in your relationships, or in any space where your dignity is at stake, then you have every right to speak up. This chapter is not about shrinking or becoming invisible. It is about separating your identity from the constant need to be acknowledged.

Validation becomes a trap when it's your only compass. When your sense of worth rises and falls based on whether someone noticed, applauded, or approved—you are handing over too much power. That power belongs to you. You are not your résumé, your bank account, your follower count, or your productivity level on any given day. And you are not defined by how many people see your value.

True internal validation comes when you stop asking, "Do they see me?" and start asking, "Do I see me? Do I accept myself even when I fall short? Even when no one is watching? Even when it's quiet?" If validation were a mirror, then it's not a stranger's eyes you need to look through; it's your own. And what you'll find is that your value doesn't increase when you win, and it doesn't disappear when you lose. You were always worthy. You've always been enough.

We often tell ourselves, "Once I get that job, I'll feel successful. Once they recognize my work, I'll feel seen. Once I'm loved, I'll feel lovable." But what if that love and recognition starts with you? And what if this whole time you were chasing a reflection that was already waiting for you to look inward?

Enoughness

Being enough isn't a prize you earn when everything in your life is in perfect alignment. It's not the reward for success, the byproduct of being loved, or a title reserved for those who have "made it." Enoughness is a declaration, and you can make it in the middle of your mess.

A few months ago, life reminded me of that truth in the most uncomfortable way. I'd just returned from traveling abroad, followed by more travel out of state. I was ready to dive back into my routines, into momentum and flow. Instead, I got sick. And not just a little under the weather; I mean knocked-out flat. It started with what looked like bug bites, and it turned out to be chickenpox. As an adult. I'll spare you the details, but let's just say I was praying for a tree to scratch my back against like a bear in the forest. Calamine lotion and sprays became my perfume. My energy was wiped out. And when I thought it couldn't get worse, the flu followed. A double hit.

I had plans. I had goals. I had schedules to keep. But my body had other ideas, and it shut everything down. I tried pushing through. I forced myself to walk and move before I was ready, and it cost me. Eventually, I surrendered. And in that surrender I found something else: the quiet truth that I was still enough. I wasn't being productive. I wasn't crushing any goals. But I was still enough simply because I exist. I was still me, still worthy, still whole—even flat on my back, covered in calamine, wondering when I'd feel like myself again.

That's what enoughness is. It's knowing that your value doesn't go on pause when life slows you down. You don't depreciate when you're not at your best. You are not less when you are healing, grieving, tired, or uncertain. You're just human.

The Gut Punch of Approval

There's a high that comes with being praised. It lights you up. For a moment, everything feels aligned. You're seen, valued, and maybe even admired. You hit that milestone. You crushed that project. You walked into a room, and they clapped. But here's what no one tells you: Applause fades. Accolades don't fill the gaps within you. And the high? It's followed by the gut punch.

The gut punch of approval is that moment after the praise wears off and you're left wondering, *What now?* You've been fed but not nourished. You've been noticed but not truly known. And if you're not careful, you begin to chase that fleeting feeling, treating it like fuel when in reality, it's smoke.

This is where disappointment settles in, when you start to realize that people may celebrate your output but not your essence. The approval you earned might not even be genuine; it could be transactional, political, obligatory. Or worse, conditional. One wrong move, one less-than-stellar day, and the applause halts. The room quiets. And you're back to wondering, *Was I ever really valued, or was I just performing?*

This is the emotional roller coaster of external validation. It seduces you with its sparkle, then leaves you aching in the aftermath. You give and give, hoping to receive something that feels permanent, but instead, it's like chasing vapor. It's exhausting.

But you don't have to live in that loop. When you start turning inward—validating your own voice, celebrating your own growth, honoring your own standards—you build something sustainable. You get off the emotional roller coaster and step into a grounded, unshakable sense of self. And that doesn't fade. That doesn't gut-punch you. That fills you.

Are you chasing the high or building the foundation? One leaves you empty; the other brings you home. Your humanity is the very proof of your strength. Don't become a victim of the validation you seek. Choose yourself. Love yourself. Validate yourself even when no one else claps, even when it's quiet, even when it's hard. Especially then.

The Emotional Aftershocks of Praise

Praise feels incredible at first. It's validating, affirming, and sometimes even euphoric. It can feel like someone has finally noticed the effort you've been putting in for years, like your work and your worth are finally aligned. But here's the hidden layer: When praise becomes your primary fuel, it also becomes your biggest vulnerability.

The aftershocks aren't always loud. Sometimes they're quiet and creeping. They show up when the applause stops. When the room doesn't clap. When no one reposts or congratulates or even notices. And suddenly, that high crashes into a low you didn't anticipate. This is the emotional debt of performance-based worth. You start second-guessing yourself. Did I peak already? Am I still enough if no one is clapping? You wonder if you need to one-up yourself just to stay relevant. You begin to craft your actions and your voice around what will get the most approval instead of what feels most authentic. And with every round of praise, the cost of your peace rises.

What's even more dangerous is you become afraid to disappoint. So you shrink, filter, and start delivering a version of yourself that feels safe. Polished. Predictable. But also disconnected from your truth. That's when the exhaustion sets in. It's soul-depleting to live out someone else's expectations of you. True validation is quiet. Steady. You feel it in the still moments, the hard days, the mirror glances when no one's watching. It's in knowing that you are worthy before the applause, beyond the praise, and regardless of the response.

The work, then, isn't to reject praise but to redefine your relationship with it. To let it be the cherry on top, not the whole cake. Let the real reward be your alignment, your growth, your grit, your joy. Praise can't build you. But presence can. Purpose can. Self-trust absolutely can. So when the applause fades—as it always does—what will you be left with?

A Quiet Realization

I remember a moment—not flashy, not headline-worthy, just honest. I had just finished speaking at an event that, on paper, looked like a dream. The kind where the crowd leans in, where every word seems to land. Afterward, I was showered with praise, handshakes, affirmations, and compliments laced with admiration. I smiled, thanked them, and took pictures. I said all the right things. But later that night in the hotel room—quiet, alone, stripped of applause—I felt empty. Not because I didn't appreciate the kindness but because I realized I had been waiting for it. I had been measuring the value of my voice by the volume of their response. And without it, even temporarily, I didn't know how to feel whole.

That shook me. Because I thought I had done the work. I thought I had learned how to affirm myself. But the truth is, external praise is seductive. It disguises itself as love. But it is incomplete. It can't hold you in the long haul. It doesn't know how to sit with you when doubt creeps in at three a.m. It doesn't pick you back up when the audience isn't clapping. It doesn't help you hit "send" on the hard emails or "post" on the unpopular truth.

That night taught me something valuable: If you let praise define you, its absence will also destroy you. So now I accept praise, but I don't rely on it. I love encouragement, but I don't hinge my worth on it. I've learned to be proud of myself in the quiet moments, in the invisible wins, in the brave choices that no one else sees. That's internal validation. And it's more than enough.

The Return to Self

Internal validation isn't a finish line you cross one triumphant day; it's a daily return to yourself. A refusal to let the world decide your value, even when it tries to hand you the script. There will always be voices (online, at work, even in your own family) that tell you you're not quite enough. Not accomplished enough. Not visible enough. Not polished, not likable, not loud, not quiet, not selfless, not ambitious—not enough. But those voices don't get to narrate your story unless you hand them the pen.

See your worth through your eyes. Choose yourself not in spite of your imperfections but because of them. Stop outsourcing your value and start living it. You don't need to prove anything. You just need to remember who you already are. That quiet truth, that unshakable center, has been there all along. And when the world goes silent and the applause fades, you'll still be standing. Rooted. Whole. Enough.

REFLECTIONS

1. *Where in my life am I still waiting for permission to feel worthy?* What area of life (career, relationships, creative pursuits) is still tied to someone else's approval?

2. *What moments in my past prove that I am already enough?* Think of times you showed up for yourself or others without external reward. What did that reveal about your character?

3. *Whose opinion have I placed above my own, and why?* Explore whether the validation you've been seeking is rooted in fear, longing, or a story that no longer serves you.

4. *What does it look like to validate myself daily?* If you believed you were enough just as you are, how would you walk into a room? How would you speak to yourself?

5. *What would I do, build, or become if I stopped waiting to be chosen?* Let this be expansive. Dream. Imagine. Own your "enoughness" with full audacity.

TAKEAWAYS

• *Internal validation is foundational. Without it, everything you build externally feels shaky.* With it, you become unshakeable.

• *The praise that once thrilled you can become the pressure that undoes you.* Seek authenticity, not applause. Choose substance over spectacle.

• *Enoughness is a decision.* You don't arrive at it; you choose it, again and again, especially on the hard days.

• *Your value is not up for debate.* Not by society, not by your past, not even by your doubts. You're not a resume, a number, or a performance.

• *When you validate yourself, you reclaim your voice.* And with that voice, you don't just speak; you lead.

Chapter Twenty Nine

Legacy

If you're always trying to be normal, you will never know how amazing you can be.
—Maya Angelou

Legacy is not merely the sum of what we accumulate in our lifetimes. It's not just the houses we build, the wealth we leave behind, or the titles we acquire. It is, in its purest form, the imprint we leave on the hearts and minds of others. The energy we share with the world. The ripple effect of our actions, our words, and our very existence.

As I think about my mother and the life she has lived, I see that her legacy isn't limited to the things she achieved. Sure, she bought the house. She bought the cars. She built a life that was both a testament to her resilience and her unwavering commitment to her goals. But what I admire most is the quiet legacy she is leaving behind.

In her sixties now, my mother moves with the energy of someone half her age. She wakes up early every morning, sets her intentions, and moves through her day without hesitation. She does this without complaint, without asking for recognition, and with a singular focus on getting things done. There is no "woe is me" in her narrative. There is no "poor me" because of the sacrifices she made. She has never viewed the price she paid as hardship. She simply viewed her sacrifices as the price of doing what she needed to do to build the life she envisioned.

When I watch her today, moving effortlessly through the crowded streets of New York, I am struck by how much of her legacy has shaped me and continues to shape those around her. Her consistency, her discipline, her refusal to complain, and her relentless drive are gifts she has passed down. It's her mindset I admire. It's the unwavering belief that anything is possible if you're willing to pay the price, to sacrifice, and to work for it.

The idea of legacy often gets clouded by superficial measures. We focus on the things that are visible, the things we can measure in dollars, titles, and awards. But the truth is, legacy is something much deeper. It is the influence we have on others. It is the character we demonstrate when faced with adversity. It is the small, seemingly insignificant choices we make daily that add up to something much greater than ourselves.

Legacy is about the stories we tell through our actions. It's about teaching others how to persevere, how to bounce back from failure, and how to love ourselves in the face of adversity. My mother never explicitly told me these things; she showed me. Her life became the blueprint, the quiet lesson that was passed down without ever being spoken aloud.

And now, as I stand here and reflect on my own journey, I see that I am in the process of building my own legacy. It's a work in progress. But it's one I'm proud of because I understand the price of the path I'm walking. I understand that I must sacrifice in order to build something worth leaving behind. Whether it's time away from my children, or enduring the emotional weight of long hours and hard work, I know it's all part of the journey.

Just as my mother's legacy was shaped by her choices, so, too, will mine be. And as I continue to build my life, I am reminded of the most important lesson she taught me:

Our legacy is not just the sum of what we accomplish, but the sum of the sacrifices we are willing to make for something that truly matters.

Creating Your Legacy

What do you want to be remembered for? What kind of impact do you want to leave on the people around you? What principles, values, and actions do you want to shape your story? The truth is, we all have the ability to create a legacy, but it requires intentionality. It requires paying the price for what matters most, even when it's hard. It requires sacrifice. But the reward is immeasurable.

As you reflect on your own legacy, ask yourself: "What am I willing to sacrifice today to create the future I want? What are the values I want to pass down to those I love? How can I live in a way that leaves a lasting imprint on this world?" Your legacy begins today, and it starts with the small, deliberate choices you make. What will you choose?

Legacy Through Impact

When we think of legacy, we often envision multimillion-dollar fortunes, renowned careers, and monuments that stand the test of time. The idea of creating something massive, something that everyone can see, tends to dominate our thoughts about what a legacy should be. But what if true legacy isn't measured by wealth, fame, or global recognition? What if it's about the ways you touch the lives of those closest to you? The quiet, consistent moments of love, support, and kindness you offer can leave a more profound imprint on the world than anything you could ever buy.

Legacy is about being known to someone in a way that changes their life. You might never be famous, but the people who cross your path will carry pieces of you with them forever. Whether it's through the lessons you teach, the encouragement you offer, or the way you show up during tough times, those small acts of impact will shape their futures in ways you'll never fully understand.

Look at the people in your life. How have they shaped you? Who are the ones who, despite not having wealth or fame, made you believe in yourself, encouraged you to grow, and walked beside you when things weren't easy?

One of the clearest examples of legacy I've witnessed is my mother-in-law. She lost her husband at a young age and was left to raise four children on her own. In a time when it would've been easy to give up, she built a thriving business and created a stable life for her family. But her greatest legacy was how she raised her children. She taught them to believe in themselves, to know their worth, and to stand tall in the face of life's challenges. Her quiet strength, her perseverance, and her unwavering dedication continue to ripple through generations. Those are the legacies that matter. And you, too, have the power to create that kind of impact.

It might feel like the world is focused on the big names and big achievements, but at the end of the day, the most powerful legacy is the one you build in your immediate circle. The difference you make in your family, your friends, and your community is what will last far beyond any physical marker of success.

We've talked about how powerful the small, seemingly insignificant moments can be. The hugs you give, the wisdom you share, and the encouragement you offer often ripple through time and affect lives in ways that you'll never fully see. But here is where we must be real with ourselves: There is nothing wrong with dreaming of a bigger legacy.

If your goal is to leave behind something that's widely recognized, something that makes an impact on a larger scale, then wonderful! Sometimes society can make us feel that our ambitions are either too small or too big, that if we're not changing the world in some major, visible way, we're not leaving any kind of legacy at all. But that couldn't be further from the truth.

If the legacy you're aiming for is something grand—something that will influence entire communities, industries, or even generations—that's something worth striving for. There's nothing wrong with wanting to build something that stands the test of time, something that can be a beacon of inspiration for others. If your ambition is to leave a mark on the world that's visible and lasting, go for it. Build it with intention, perseverance, and heart. There is no rule that says we can't aim for greatness in our own unique way.

Some legacies are built with the hopes of changing the world for the better on a global scale. We see that with leaders, innovators, and creators who dedicate their lives to transforming industries, lifting others, and making life better for countless people. This kind of legacy is often harder to see while it's being built, but it is no less valuable.

What's important is recognizing that both paths—the quiet, intimate impact and the larger, more visible legacy—are worthy. You can choose the kind of legacy that feels right to you. Whether you want to be remembered by the people you've directly impacted in your life, or you dream of creating something that will change the course of history, both are valid goals. The key is aligning your actions with your vision, and ensuring that your legacy is one you can be proud of.

When we get caught up in comparing our legacies to others, we forget that legacy is deeply personal. It's about the values you want to instill, the difference you hope to make, and the kind of person you aim to be. And at the end of the day, it's about how you feel about the life you've lived. If you feel fulfilled by the impact you've made, and the way you've shown up for others, that's a legacy that can never be taken away.

What's essential is that you acknowledge what feels most authentic to you. Whether your legacy takes the form of deeply personal, behind-the-scenes work or a more public, visible impact, the measure of a meaningful life is not in comparison but in the intention behind your actions.

REFLECTIONS

As we think about the legacy we want to leave, I encourage you to ask yourself the following:

1. What kind of legacy do I want to leave behind? How do I want to be remembered by the people closest to me?

2. Am I content with creating a legacy that impacts my immediate circle, or do I dream of something larger? How can I take the next step toward that vision?

3. What values do I want to pass on, and how can I embody those values in my daily life?

4. How do I define success in terms of legacy, and how can I measure it not just by accolades but by the lives I've touched?

There is no one right way to build a legacy. It's about what aligns with your heart and the mark you want to leave on the world. Embrace it.

TAKEAWAYS

- *To the mom who feels overwhelmed, who balances a career, kids, and life's demands, I see you. I know you feel like there is not enough time in the day.* I know the days when you feel like you are not enough or doing enough. But you are more than enough. You've already shown incredible strength by simply getting through each day.

- *Imagine if you embraced that possibility mindset—not just for your own dreams but for your legacy, for the impact you'll have on the world and on your kids.* You can do more than survive; you can thrive. Whether it's through the moments you give to your children, the small acts of kindness to those around you, or the big dreams you're working towards, everything you do leaves a mark.

- *Your legacy doesn't have to be built on the grand gestures or the accolades you might see others get.* It's built in the day-to-day moments, in how you show up, in how you lead your family, how you empower others. Your impact is priceless.

- *The timing may never feel perfect. Life is always full, always busy.* But you don't need the stars to align to begin shaping your legacy. It starts with one small step, one intentional choice. Don't wait. Start now!

● *Your legacy is waiting to be written, and you are the author.* You have everything inside of you to make it happen. Keep going, keep believing, and keep showing up. The world is waiting for you to take that step.

Chapter Thirty

Take Center Stage!

There's no prerequisites to worthiness. You're born worthy, and I think that's a message a lot of women need to hear.
—Viola Davis

There are women whose names are never written in history books, who never stood behind podiums or amassed crowds, and yet their lives speak louder than the loudest microphone ever could. My maternal grandmother, Jessie Durga Bharat, was one of those women. I never had the chance to truly know her. She passed away when I was just a baby. But her presence still lingers—not in photographs or plaques, but in the way people speak of her. She was soft, kind, and deeply compassionate. She didn't have much by way of material possessions, but she poured out what she did have—her

Satya V. Nauth

time, her tenderness, her listening ear—into the lives of others. Her poise, servitude, and grace were the quiet threads she used to weave her life. And generations later, we still feel it.

My paternal grandmother, Jagpattie Ramnauth, on the other hand, was a force to be reckoned with. Bold, loud, unapologetic in the way she showed up for life. She grew up poor but worked hard—tilling the land, cleaning trenches, selling produce at the market, doing whatever it took to support her family and uplift her community. After my father passed, it was her strength we leaned on often. People respected her deeply because she gave all she had. She was the kind of woman who stamped her presence into the earth beneath her feet.

These women (though vastly different) didn't wait for a spotlight. They made one with their lives. And that's what I want you to see: Taking center stage isn't always about standing on platforms or commanding attention. Sometimes it looks like ordinary women who dare to live fully in their truth.

The Power of Showing Up

My good friend Monique is a mother in her early thirties, juggling two kids, a demanding job, and the quiet ache of dreams she hasn't had time to chase. Her story isn't uncommon, but it's one we don't hear about enough. One morning started like all the others. She woke up feeling like she hadn't slept at all. The baby had been up twice in the night, her five-year-old wet the bed, and the kitchen still smelled faintly like burnt toast from yesterday's chaotic morning. It was only 6:47 a.m., and already she was exhausted.

She shuffled to the kitchen with one eye open, trying to find a clean mug. Her toddler spilled cereal on the floor, and her phone buzzed with back-to-back emails about work she hadn't finished. She still needed to prep for that parent-teacher conference, finish a report, and somehow get herself ready to face the world. It felt like everything and everyone needed a piece of her. She didn't have the answers. But she paused. Right there in the mess, she exhaled long enough to hear herself think: *What if this doesn't have to be the end of me? What if there is still something beautiful waiting for me in the middle of this madness?*

That moment didn't fix everything. But it gave her something essential: a reset. A shift. A flicker of power in a day that often felt powerless. Sometimes, that's the beginning of everything. That's when she took her first step toward center stage out of courage.

Trusting Your Voice and Decisions

In Japanese tradition, *kotodama* means "the spirit of words," and is the belief that language has soul and spoken words carry energy capable of transforming the world. I believe that same power lives in your voice. The words you speak to others—and even more importantly, the ones you utter to yourself—can shape how you live. But somewhere along the way, many women were taught to silence themselves. To second-guess. To defer. To apologize.

Your voice was never meant to stay quiet. You don't need perfect wording or permission. You just need to believe that what's stirring in you—the questions, the clarity, the knowing—is worth trusting. There is power in honoring your own rhythm. Power in speaking your truth, even if your voice shakes when it leaves your lips. Let your yes mean something. Let your no stand tall. Let your voice be the compass, not the echo.

Hildegard of Bingen was a twelfth-century nun who spent much of her early life suppressing the visions, music, and spiritual insights she received. At a time when women were forbidden from speaking boldly (especially about matters of divinity), she held her voice in silence. But in her forties, something shifted. The call inside her grew louder than the fear outside. She chose to speak. When she did, she poured out songs, writings, visions, and wisdom that changed lives—and that we still study today. She trusted the truth within her and gave it space to rise.

You don't have to wait either. You don't need credentials to believe your inner knowing. You don't need permission to say, "This is who I am, and this is what I see. "The world may not understand your voice right away, but it will remember your courage.

You are probably not a nun. And it's definitely not the twelfth century anymore. But even in 2025, too many women still feel like their voices have been buried beneath expectations, roles, and silence. It's time. Time to raise your voice.

Whole, Not Perfect

For years, we've been taught to perform. To polish. To perfect. We smooth over the hard parts of our stories and hide the cracks that feel too jagged to name. We smile when we're breaking. We say "I'm fine "when we're unraveling. And slowly, we begin to believe the only version of us that's worthy is the edited one. But taking center stage means stepping out as is—unfiltered, unpolished, and unafraid to be whole.

Wholeness means bringing your contradictions with you. It means honoring your grief and your joy, your weariness and your wonder. It means being big when the world wants you small. It means not slicing yourself into pieces just to fit someone else's idea of *enough*.

There is a beautiful Japanese art called *kintsugi*, where broken pottery is repaired with gold. Instead of hiding the cracks, it highlights them. The breaks don't make the vessel worthless; they make it more precious. More powerful. More true. That's the kind of life you're allowed to build. One where you stop pretending you were never hurt and instead show that healing is part of the design. So no more hiding the pieces. Let them shine.

Unapologetic, Unequivocal Confidence

Confidence does not mean having it all figured out. It means standing in who you are, even when you're still becoming. It's the quiet knowing that you don't have to shrink to be worthy. That your power doesn't need softening. That your truth doesn't require permission. You don't owe the world a diluted version of yourself. You don't need to second-guess your presence in the room.

Your voice belongs there. Your ideas belong there. You belong there.

Unapologetic, unequivocal confidence is *alignment*. It's knowing that what you carry matters, and refusing to bury it for the comfort of others. It's saying, "This is who I am" without blinking. Some people won't understand your boldness. You were made to be powerful. And the more you witness yourself—your truth, your fire, your softness—the more magnetic you become. Your softness doesn't need hardening. Your strength doesn't need softening. Your *trueness* just needs the spotlight.

Confidence walks in with peace, with presence, and with the kind of power that makes people sit up straighter because your being commands it. This is what taking center stage looks like. Not performing. Not pleasing. Just showing up whole and sure.

Now It's Your Turn

You've spent years in the wings—holding it all together, pouring into others, doubting whether you were ever enough. But you were never meant to stay behind the curtains. You've earned this moment. This is the part of your story where the curtain rises. Where you stop waiting for the "right time" and realize *you* are the right time. You have done the quiet work. You have become the steady center in a world that often spins. And now, it's your turn to be seen. Fully. Boldly. Unapologetically.

Remember, it's presence over perfection. The world needs your truth. Your story. Your voice. Your scars. Your wholeness. Your imperfect *perfection*. And it starts with one brave step toward the light. One bold reach to the crown. So stand tall. Take a breath. Mom, it's time to take center stage.

REFLECTIONS

The Final Note

This book serves as a mirror. A reminder. A reclaiming. Hopefully, you have remembered who you are and begun to turn corners in your life. You will not go back to hiding. You will not question your worth. You will not shrink into the background.

Ask yourself these questions boldly and without apology:

- What part of me have I been dimming that's finally ready to shine?

- When did I start believing I needed permission to want more?

- Where in my life have I been performing instead of showing up whole?

- What would it look like to lead with trust instead of fear?

- If I stopped abandoning myself, what kind of woman would I become?

- What will my children (or the people I love) remember when they speak my name?

- Am I ready to take center stage and elevate my life?

TAKEAWAYS

- *This is your moment.* This is not a rehearsal. It is in the way you love. The way you show up. The way you refuse to quit. And from this moment forward, it is in the way you choose yourself—boldly, without apology.

- *You are not just building something.* You are something. And the world is better because you are in it.

- *Own your power.* Own your voice. Tell your story. Change the room when you enter it. You've earned it. And I believe you can because I already know you will.

- *You are no longer waiting for permission or validation.* You are trusting your voice, your pace, and your power. That's what it means to take center stage.

- *Taking center stage is about living whole, not fragmented or hidden.* But seen, safe, and fully present in your own life.

Acknowledgments

First and foremost, this book has been a labor of love over the past year. I thank my family for their unwavering support because without them, this would not have been possible.

To my beta readers and critique partners, who toiled over thousands of words and gave me honest, thoughtful feedback—I am forever grateful.

To my editor, Jenna Love Schrader, who has been a beacon of hope, support, and insight. You poured into me with care and challenged me to grow. For that, my words of thanks will never be enough.

And finally, I cannot end without honoring the greater light that has always guided me through trials, through tribulations, and ultimately, into my own. That light has led me here. To center stage.

Notes

Chapter 2: Supermom Habits

1. "Suppressing Negative Thoughts May Be Good for Mental Health After All," Sept. 20, 2023, University of Cambridge, last accessed May 26, 2025, https://www.cam.ac.uk/research/news/suppressing-negative-thoughts-good-for-mental-health.

Chapter 12: The Power of Now

1. Janet Dailey, GoodReads, https://www.goodreads.com/quotes/162915-someday-is-not-a-day-of-the-week.

Chapter 15: The Window of Self-Discovery

1. Luft, J. H., & Ingham, H. (1955), "The Johari Window: A graphic model for interpersonal awareness," Presented at the Western Training Laboratory in Group Development, UCLA.

2. Marie Forleo, *Everything Is Figureoutable: One Simple Belief to Create Unstoppable Success* (Portfolio, 2019).

Satya V. Nauth is a writer, entrepreneur, and personal growth advocate with a background in marketing, leadership development, and the short-term rental industry. She lives in Florida with her family, where life is full, vibrant, and always a little bit messy—in the best way.

When she's not writing or running her business, you'll likely find her with a book in hand or walking under the evening sky, reflecting on life's many layers. She believes in the quiet power of intentional living, the boldness of taking center stage, and the beauty of stories that speak the unspoken truths of modern womanhood.

Mom Take Center Stage is her debut book, written for every woman who is ready to stop shrinking and start shining.

Continue Taking Center Stage

You've reached the end—but this is just the beginning of your bold, purpose-filled journey.

Here's how you can keep showing up for your life—and for yourself:

✨ Join the Movement

Sign up for tools, reflections, and first access to what's next.

SatyaNauth.com (https://satyanauth.com) or go there directly by scanning the QR code:

🎤 Invite Me to Speak

Want to bring the message of *Mom Take Center Stage* to your community, group, or event?

➤ SatyaNauth.com (https://satyanauth.com/contact/)

📖 Leave a Review

Your voice matters. Share your thoughts and help more moms find this book.

➤ https://a.co/d/0G56pMm

➤ https://books2read.com/u/baMdry

💬 Connect and Share

Follow along on:

Instagram/Tik Tok: @Satya_Nauth

Facebook: https://facebook.com/satya.nauth.3

Email: MomTakeCenterStage@gmail.com

Tag #MomTakeCenterStage to let the world see how you're taking the lead.

You're not just a reader—you're part of a movement. And this is your moment.

Coming Soon...

Mom Takes Center Stage

A Bold, Unapologetic, Unfiltered Journal for Moms Ready to Reclaim the Spotlight

You've spent enough time backstage.

This journal isn't here to fix you.

It's here to *free* you.

To give you a space that's finally, fully yours—to speak your truth, write your rage, capture your dreams, and name the things no one else can see but you.

It's raw. It's real. It's yours.

And it's for the mom who's ready to stop shrinking, stop apologizing, and start showing up—louder, bolder, and more fully herself than ever before.

A Few Prompts to Get You Started

1. What would I do differently today if I stopped asking for permission?

Let it out without editing. What's the move you're not making yet?

2. Where have I been silent when I should have spoken?

This isn't about shame. It's about clarity—and the power of your voice.

3. What does taking center stage look like in my everyday life?

Don't overthink it. Write the small, radical acts that put you back in the spotlight.

4. What part of myself have I been hiding to make others more comfortable?

Say it. Name it. Reclaim it.

5. I'm most magnetic when I…

Fill in the blank—again and again. Let it flow.

Ready for More?

The full journal is coming soon.

Sign up at SatyaNauth.com (https://satyanauth.com) to be the first to know when it launches—and get exclusive launch-week bonuses just for this community.

Satya V. Nauth